常 识

（中英双语彩插本）

〔美〕托马斯·潘恩 著 余瑾 译

中华书局

图书在版编目（CIP）数据

常识（中英双语彩插本）/（美）潘恩（Paine, T.）著；余瑾译．—北京：中华书局，2013.7（2015.11 重印）
（国民阅读经典）
ISBN 978－7－101－09385－8

Ⅰ．常… Ⅱ．①潘…②余… Ⅲ．政治思想史－美国－近代 Ⅳ. D097. 124

中国版本图书馆 CIP 数据核字（2013）第 113456 号

书　　名	常识（中英双语彩插本）
著　　者	〔美〕托马斯·潘恩
译　　者	余　瑾
丛 书 名	国民阅读经典
责任编辑	林玉萍
装帧设计	毛　淳
出版发行	中华书局
	（北京市丰台区太平桥西里 38 号　100073）
	http://www.zhbc.com.cn
	E-mail:zhbc@ zhbc.com.cn
印　　刷	北京天来印务有限公司
版　　次	2013 年 7 月北京第 1 版
	2015 年 11 月北京第 2 次印刷
规　　格	开本/880×1230 毫米　1/32
	印张 6　插页 8　字数 108 千字
印　　数	10001－14000 册
国际书号	ISBN 978－7－101－09385－8
定　　价	18.00 元

托马斯·潘恩

Wolcott 67:1

PLAIN TRUTH;

ADDRESSED TO THE

INHABITANTS

O F

AMERICA,

Containing, Remarks

ON A LATE PAMPHLET,

entitled

COMMON SENSE:

Wherein are shewn, that the Scheme of INDEPENDENCE
is Ruinous, Delusive, and Impracticable: That were
the Author's Asseverations, Respecting the Power of
AMERICA, as Real as Nugatory; Reconciliation on
liberal Principles with GREAT BRITAIN, would be
exalted Policy: And that circumstanced as we are,
Permanent Liberty, and True Happiness, can only be
obtained, by HONORABLE CONNECTIONS,
with that Kingdom.

WRITTEN BY CANDIDUS.

~~Doct~~ ~~*Smith of Phila.*~~

Will ye turn from flattery, and attend to this Side.?

There TRUTH, unlicenc'd, walks; and dares accost
Even Kings themselves, the Monarchs of the Free!
THOMSON on the Liberties of BRITAIN.

PHILADELPHIA:
Printed, and Sold, by R. BELL, in Third-Street.

MDCCLXXVI.

《常识》书影

GEORGE III.
King of Great Britain &c.

英王乔治三世

18 世纪 70 年代的漫画，北美这匹马正将骑手乔治三世摔下马

1770 年波士顿大屠杀

波士顿倾茶事件

1775 年 3 月帕特里克·亨利大声疾呼："不自由，毋宁死！"

莱克星敦的枪声

邦克山战役

美国独立战争时期大陆军之陆军

华盛顿被任命为大陆军总司令

美国独立战争时期的海军英雄：
琼斯、默里、戴尔、巴里、普雷布尔、比德尔

北美民兵

走向战场的北美战士

草拟《独立宣言》

签署《独立宣言》

出版说明

　　在二十一世纪的当代中国，国民的阅读生活中最迫切的事情是什么？我们的回答是：阅读经典！

　　在承担着国民基础知识体系构建的中国基础教育被功利和应试扭曲了的今天，我们要阅读经典；当数字化、网络化带来的"信息爆炸"占领人们的头脑、占用人们的时间时，我们要阅读经典；当中华民族迈向和平崛起、民族复兴的伟大征程时，我们更要阅读经典。

　　经典是我们知识体系的根基，是精神世界的家园，是走向未来的起点。这就是我们编选这套《国民阅读经典》丛书的缘起，也因此决定了这套丛书的几个特点：

　　首先，入选的经典是指古今中外人文社科领域的名著。世界的眼光、历史的观点和中国的根基，是我们编选这套丛书的三个基本的立足点。

第二，入选的经典，不是指某时某地某一专业领域之内的重要著作，而是指历经岁月的淘洗、汇聚人类最重要的精神创造和知识积累的基础名著，都是人人应读、必读和常读的名著。我们从中精选出一百部，分辑出版。

第三，入选的经典，我们坚持优中选优的原则，尽量选择最好的版本，选择最好的注本或译本。

我们真诚地希望，这套经典丛书能够进入你的生活，相伴你的左右。

中华书局编辑部

二〇一二年四月

目录

Common Sense

Common Sense

Introduction / 83

Of the Origin and Design of Government in General, with

　　Concise Remarks on the English Constitution / 85

译者序

　　很多年前，在新英格兰腹地达慕思大学哥特风格的图书馆中，看到手里"美国政治思想史"的课程安排，我不禁一片茫然——第一课竟将开始于我从未听说过的托马斯·潘恩和他的《常识》。潘恩是谁？《常识》又是本什么样的书？

　　在我们的教科书中，甚至是高等学府"美国历史"专题课上，美国历史都是肇始于华盛顿、富兰克林、杰斐逊、汉密尔顿这些璀璨耀眼的名字和鼎鼎大名的《独立宣言》。为什么当代美国最著名的自由主义知识分子却将潘恩的《常识》视为这个世界头号强国的思想基石和理论起点？为什么教授会在课堂上饱含激情地大段背诵《常识》？很久之后回想这一切，我才真切地意识到，潘恩的《常识》是美国精神的基座，已经深深地契入了美国人的基因中，所以才经常被我们这些外国人在走马观花中忽略。事实上，正是潘恩和《常识》缔造了美国，而美利坚合众国之名也是出自潘恩之手。

托马斯·潘恩（Thomas Paine，1737—1809），这个出生于裁缝之家的英国人传奇般地参加并极大地推动了18世纪，也是历史上最伟大的三场革命：美国独立战争、法国大革命和英国宪章运动。他撰写了大量政论文章和专著，启蒙、鼓动了徘徊在现代文明起点的欧美民众。《常识》一书就是他的成名作和代表作。

1774年，在本杰明·富兰克林的帮助下，潘恩踏上了北美大陆，定居费城。1776年1月，就在北美殖民地人民渐渐开始接受独立主张的时候，潘恩在费城化名"英国人"出版了《常识》，在这片新大陆上第一次明确呼喊出要求脱离英国控制而独立的愿望。该书出版后大受欢迎，北美战士几乎人手一册，并迅速在各国广泛流传，被誉为"世界上第一本真正意义上的畅销书"，是《圣经》之后影响力最大、影响范围最广的一本书。

《常识》的伟大之处不仅仅在于首次提出北美独立的要求，更重要的是，潘恩高瞻远瞩地为独立之后的北美规划了一条切实可行的政治道路，不但引导美国走上了民主共和之路，而且滋养了整个西方现代政治文明进程。潘恩在书中表现出超越时代的远见卓识，一针见血地指出君主制和世袭继承的种种弊端，冷静地分析了政府的起源与本质，并细致缜密地设计出一套民主代议制度。书中既有气势磅礴的谴责、呼吁，又有理性冷静的分析、构建，寥寥数万言，却字字珠玑。《常识》的激情与睿智被《独立宣言》全盘吸收，成为美国独立及建国的纲领和基石。

本书以《常识》第三版为底本译出，并收录潘恩驳斥和解主张的《致贵格会教徒书》为附录，以期更全面地展示潘恩的思想。书中涉及不少西方文化的背景知识，如多处引用《圣经》，时常提及18世纪的英国政治家和风靡一时的学者等。这对18世纪中后期的欧美人来说是"常识"，但对当代中国读者来说，却是一条深深的鸿沟。为了扫清阅读障碍，译者特意撰写了大量注释，以帮助读者弄清语义背景、相关人物和事件。近些年来，随着对西方文化了解的不断加深，潘恩和《常识》开始频频出现在国内学者的口头与笔端；激情四溢而又理性睿智的《常识》也被不少学校和培训机构作为英文朗读、背诵的材料之一。因此，书后特附上《常识》的英文原文，以便读者能够领略到原文的风采。

译者
2013 年 3 月

引　言

　　或许，本书所表达的观点尚未风靡一时并获得广泛的赞同。长期以来，我们习惯径直接受，不去质疑。这种惯性不但使得事情表面上看起来似乎正确，而且往往从提出质疑之初就会引起捍卫传统的强大舆论。但是，争论很快就会平息。时间比理性更能说服人改弦更张。

　　长期地、为所欲为地滥用使权力的正当性受到质疑（其他事情亦是如此。如果受压迫者从未忍无可忍，揭竿而起讨要公道，一切可能永远不会改变）。英国国王拥有自己的权利，同时还支持议会拥有他所谓的"他们的"权利。二者联手残酷压榨这个国家的善良民众。因此，人民拥有不容置疑的基本权利去质疑他们声称拥有的权利，并且有权拒绝任何一方篡夺这些权利。

　　笔者将在后文中尽力避免个人化的东西，当然，对个人的恭维和指责也不会在行文中出现。睿智之人和成功之士不需要依靠一本小册子的成功。我们也不需要费尽心思强迫那些不明智或不友好的人改换门庭，他们会自然消解。

在很大程度上，北美的事业就是全人类的事业。许多具有普遍意义的（非地方性的）因素已经或者即将出现，它们势必会影响热爱人类的人们所信奉的原则并触动他们的心弦。燃起战火使一个国家鸡犬不留、挑战天赋之人权并将人权捍卫者斩尽杀绝——所有被上天赋予感知力的人都不会对这些暴行无动于衷，不论时人如何评说，**笔者**就是这些人中的一员。

1776 年 2 月 14 日于费城

第一章　综论政府的起源与目的并简评英国政体

社会为我们的欲望所造就，政府则由我们的邪恶所产生。前者使我们同心协力，积极地提升我们的幸福感；后者通过抑制罪行而提升幸福感。

有些作家将政府与社会混为一谈，以致搞得二者之间没有什么不同，甚或完全没有区别。事实上，它们不但有区别，而且起源就截然不同。社会为我们的欲望所造就，政府则由我们的邪恶所产生。前者使我们同心协力，积极地提升我们的幸福感；后者通过抑制罪行而提升幸福感。一个鼓励交流，另一个创立区别；前一个是奖励者，后一个是惩罚者。

在任何情况下，社会都是福祉。但是，即便最好的政府，也不过是必要的恶；最坏的政府则是令人无法容忍的恶。这是因为，当我们遭受苦难，或者承受种种政府导致的、我们原本以为只有在无政府国家才会遇到的灾祸时，会意识到正是我们自己养虎为患，反受其噬而分外痛苦。政府就像是衣服，是失去天真纯朴的标志；帝王的宫殿建立在天堂亭台的废墟之上。

如果人们总是完全彻底、始终如一、毫不抗拒地按照良心的冲动行事，就根本不需要其他立法者。但是，事实恰恰相反，政府成为一种必要的选择。人们一贯秉持的两害相权取其轻的谨慎促使他们认识到，有必要放弃一部分财产来保全剩余的。因此，既然安全是政府的真正意图和目的，那么，毋庸置疑，任何看起来最有可能保证我们安全的、花费最少收益最大的政体形式，就是最好的选择。

为了清楚而正确地理解政府的意图和目的，我们假定一小群人在地球上某个荒僻角落安顿下来，与世隔绝。他们代表了任何国家或者说就是全世界的首批居民。在这种天然的自由状态下，社会将是进入他们脑海中的第一个念头，而种种动机也会促使他们向着这个方向努力。个人的力量无法满足自己的各种欲望，再加上心理上也难以忍受长期的孤独，因此，人很快被迫寻求别人的帮助和慰藉；而对方也有同样的需求。四五个人通力合作就可以在荒野之中盖起一座过得去的房子，而单独一人可能终其一生也无所作为。他砍倒了大树，却无力搬运；就是运走了，也无法将之竖立起来；与此同时，饥饿会迫使他放下手头的工作。每一种不同的欲望都用不同的方式驱使他、搅扰他。疾病，甚至灾祸都可能致人于死地，尽管它们本身可能并不致命，但却会令人丧失生活能力，陷入半死不活的境地。

如此一来，需求就像引力似的，很快使这些新移民组成了社会，而社会中的互惠福祉也接踵而至。只要人们公平互助，法律和政府就毫无用处。但是，除了天堂，没有什么能免于邪恶的玷污。所以，在同心协力、相互扶持度过了移民初期的艰难之后，人们不可避免地懈怠了自己的责任，减弱了彼此的联系，社会凝聚力便减弱了。这说明，有必要建立某种形式的政府来弥补道德的缺陷。

某棵近便适用的大树就是他们的议事堂。全体移民都可以聚在树下商议公共事务。很有可能，他们最初的法律以"守则"为名，以公众的鄙视唾弃作为处罚。在这最早的议会中，每个人都根据天赋权利拥有一个席位。

起初，当移民人数很少，居所临近，议题寥寥无几且琐碎平常的时候，每个人都参与讨论所有的问题。此后，随着移民区的发展，公众关注的议题也随之增加；而居住距离也将居民们分隔开来。因此，所有人就每一个议题集会的方式就变得非常不便。于是，从全体人员中选出若干来负责立法事务就成为一种方便可行的办法。这些代表应该与全体选民一体同心，并且应像全体人员都与会那样行事。如果移民区继续发展，代表人数则应增加；每一部分人的利益都应该得到关照。所以，最好的办法是将移民区划分为若干适当的部分，每个部分选派适当数量的代表。代表们不得谋求与选民无关的个人利益。出于审慎的考虑，经常举行选举确是明智之举。如果当选者可能会在几个月后落选，再次成为平头百姓，他们就会在任期内慎重行事。这一措施有效保证了当选者对选民的忠诚。经常性选举也将建立起社区内各部分的共同利益，它们会自然而然地相互扶持；而政府的力量和被管理者的幸福正是建立在此基础上（而不是建立在毫无意义的国王名号上）。

这便是政府的起源，换句话说，就是因为道德无力约束世界而产生的一种必要的管理模式；这其中也包含了政府的意图和目的，即自由和安全。尽管我们的眼睛可能被白雪所迷眩，我们的耳朵可能被声音所欺骗，尽管我们的意愿可能被偏见所扭曲，我们的认知可能被利益所蒙蔽，但是，自然和理性的诚恳声音告诉我们：这是正确的。

我依据一条无法推翻的自然原则得出了对政体的看法：即，事情越简单就越不容易被搞乱，即便弄乱了也更容易修正。我将据此原则对受到交口吹捧的英国政体进行评论。毫无疑问，在制定它的那个黑暗的奴隶时代，英国政体是卓然超群的。在整个世界暴政横行的时候，尽量不背离这种政体，也是一种不错的出路。但是，显而易见，它并不完善，可能会受到暴乱的侵扰，并且不能履行它表面上的承诺。

专制政府（尽管这是人性的耻辱）自有其优点：它们很简单。如果人们遭受苦难，他们既知道暴行来自何处，也清楚救治的办法，不会被各种各样的原因和解决方案弄得手忙脚乱。但是，英国政体太过复杂，以致国家长期遭受荼毒而未能发现问题所在。有人说问题在这儿，有人说在那儿，每个政治医生都开出不同的药方。

我知道，要克服狭隘的或长期存在的偏见很困难，但是，如果我们仔细检视英国政体的组成，就会发现它不过是混合了一些新鲜的共和制元素的两种古老暴政的卑劣遗骸。

首先是以国王为代表的君主政体的残余。

其次是以上议院为代表的贵族政治的残余。

再次是以下议院为代表的新的共和制元素；而英国的自由全赖其德行。

前两者是世袭的，与民众无关；而且，从政体的角度看，它们与国家的自由毫无干系。

认为英国政体是三权分立、互相制约的观点真是滑稽可笑——这种说法要么是空洞暧昧，毫无意义；要么是彻头彻尾的自相矛盾。

认为下议院制约王权的观点假设了两个先决条件：

第一，国王在未受监督的情况下是不可信任的；换句话说，对绝对权力的渴求是君主制的先天疾病。

第二，出于制约王权的目的，下议院议员要么比国王更聪明，要么更值得信赖。

这么一个政体先是使下议院拥有通过控制政府开支来制约

国王的权力，然后又赋予国王通过驳回其议案而制约下议院的权力。这不是在暗示，国王比那些原本应比他聪明的人更聪明吗？多么荒谬无稽！

君主制中存在一些自相矛盾的东西。它首先令一个人孤陋寡闻，然后让他全权解决那些需要高超判断力的问题。也就是说，国王的身份使其游离于世外，但国王的职责却要求他洞悉世事。这些不合常理的矛盾对立、抵消牵制，证明了国王的整个存在的荒谬绝伦、无用无益。

有些论者曾经这样解释英国政体，他们说，国王是一方，民众是另一方；上议院代表国王的利益，下议院代表民众的利益。这种区分会导致议会内部分裂，自相对立。尽管其措辞华美，但仔细推敲起来就会发现其实内容空洞暧昧。用来描述不存在的事物，或是极其不可思议而无法描述的事物的优美辞章仅仅是悦耳的音节，并不能传达有效信息。这种情况屡见不鲜。上述观点包含了一个先决问题，也就是说，国王是怎么拥有了民众不敢信任，又时时需要加以制约的权力？这种权力绝非得自明智的人民；而且，任何需要制约的权力也不可能来自上帝，但宪法条文却认定这样的权力确实存在。

显然，这样的宪法条文不可能得到履行，而且，通过这种方法既不能，也不会达到目的。这整个儿就是自我毁灭。既然较重的砝码能够带起较轻的物品，既然一部机器的所有轮子都是由一个轮子驱动，我们只需要知道，在这个政体内哪种权力最重要，也就是确定具有决定性作用的因素。尽管其他权力或是其中的某些要素可能阻碍或减慢整体运行，但是，只要没能使之停止，那就是徒劳无功。第一推动力①终有自己的运行方式，速度上的不足将由时间来补偿。

国王在英国政体中拥有绝对的权力。这一点是不言自明的。显而易见，国王仅仅作为地位和年金的提供者就获得了一切。尽管我们已经足够聪明地对君主专制关门落锁，但同时却愚蠢地让国王手握钥匙。

英国人热爱他们自己的由国王、上议院、下议院组成的政府。这种偏见一半出于民族自豪感，一半出于理性；或者前者所占比重更多。毫无疑问，个人在英国比在其他某些国家更安全。但是，与法国一样，国王的意志也是英国土地上的法律；唯一的区别是，英国的法律不是出自国王之口，而是以议会法案这种最令人敬畏的形式颁示天下。查理一世②的命运只不过使国王们更加狡猾，而不是更加正直。

因此，抛开所有形式、方法方面的民族自豪感与偏见，实实

---

① 指王权。——译者注（后面的注释如未特别注明，则皆为译者注）

② 查理一世（1600—1649），英国国王，1625 年即位。他在位期间与议会争执不断，并挑起英国内战。1649 年，议会对战败的查理一世进行审判，并判处死刑。他是唯一一位被处死的英国国王。

在在的真理是：英国国王之所以不像土耳其国王那样残暴，并不是因为政体，而是因为人民的素质。

此时此刻，探讨英国政体的结构性错误是非常必要的。在受到某种有强烈倾向的偏好的影响时，我们很难公允行事。同样道理，当我们固执己见的时候，也就丧失了自知之明。一个迷恋娼妓的男人，没有资格挑选或评价妻子；同理而言，对某个腐朽政体的偏爱，也使得我们无法辨别出好政体。

第二章　论君主制与世袭继承

因为人人生而平等，所以没有人生来就有权给予自己的家族超越其他家族的永久优先权。

在宇宙秩序中，人人生而平等；只是后来的某些情状制造了不平等。在很大程度上，贫富差距应当对此负责，而根本不必诿过于"压迫"、"贪婪"这些刺耳难听的字眼儿。压迫通常是富有的结果，但很少或者可以说从来都不是致富的手段。尽管贪婪使人免于穷困，但又往往使人胆小畏怯而不能发家。

不过，世界上还存在另外一种根本无法用自然的、宗教的原因解释的更大的差别，即，**国王**与**臣民**之间的区分。男人与女人是自然呈现的区别，善与恶是上天定义的区别。可是，一群人怎么会生下来就高高在上，像某个新物种那样超凡卓著？这个问题值得我们探讨，看看他们究竟是人类幸福的源泉，还是苦难的根源？

根据《圣经》记载，古时候没有国王。结果就是，当时世界上没有战争。而现在，正是国王们的傲慢使人类陷入混乱之中。近一个世纪以来，没有国王的荷兰①比欧洲其他任何君主国都享有更多的和平。历史也支持这种论断，因为随着以色列君王时代的开启而消失的那种早期部族时代的平静的乡村生活自有其幸福所在。

君主制是异教徒的发明，以色列人后来照搬复制。这是魔鬼在推进偶像崇拜过程中最成功的创造。异教徒将故去的先王尊为神灵，基督教世界则更进一步，奉尚在人世的国王为神。将"神圣的陛下"这样的头衔用在一个转瞬即逝的得志小人身上真是莫大的亵渎。

将一个人高高捧起凌驾于众人之上，这既有悖于天赋的平等权利，也无法在《圣经》中找到论据来自圆其说。正像基甸②和先知撒母耳③所传布的，全能全知的上帝明确不赞成以国王为首

---

① 指 1581—1795 年的荷兰共和国，又称联省共和国。这段时间也是历史上著名的荷兰黄金时代。

② 基甸，古代以色列士师，事略见于《旧约·士师记》。他遵照上帝的指示，拆毁了巴力神的祭坛，并带领 300 名勇士大败米甸大军，使以色列人得享数十年太平。以色列人想拥立他为王，但他拒绝了；关于"士师"，请见第 13 页注②的说明。

③ 撒母耳，古代以色列祭司、先知，其名意为"神听到了"。他生于公元前 11 世纪，处在以色列从士师时代到君王时代的转折时期，是以色列进入君王时代之前最后一位手握重权的士师，也是以色列立国后的第一位先知。他先后膏立扫罗和大卫为王，被以色列人视为民族英雄，也是《圣经》中极少数几个未受指摘的人物之一。

脑的政府。在君主制国家里，《圣经》中所有反对君主制的内容统统被巧妙地掩盖起来。但是，它们无疑值得尚未组成政府的国家的关注。虽然"凯撒的归凯撒"①是世俗宫廷所采用的《圣经》教义，但它并不支持君主制，因为当时的以色列人还没有国王，只是罗马人的藩属而已。

从摩西讲述的创世起，直到以色列人在集体迷茫中请立国王，时间大概过去了3000年。除去上帝直接插手干预的特例之外，以色列人的政体一直是由一名士师②与部落长老们共治的共和制形式。他们不但没有国王，而且认为，除了我主耶和华之外，承认任何凡人拥有国王头衔都是罪恶。倘若认真反思对君王的个人崇拜，我们就会发现，一贯珍惜名誉的万能的上帝绝对不会赞成君主制这种大不敬地侵犯上天特权的政体。

在《圣经》中，君主制被列为以色列人的罪恶之一，他们因此而受到诅咒。这段历史值得我们略作回顾。

---

① 此话出自《新约》，原文作："凯撒的归凯撒，上帝的归上帝。"一般认为，此言表达了政教分离的思想，即，凯撒代表了世俗生活和世俗权力，上帝代表了精神生活和宗教权力。也有些人认为，这句话的意思是，要求人们恪守本分，做好分内之事，以实现社会的安定祥和。

② 士师是古代以色列集宗教、政治、军事大权于一身的领袖。据《旧约·士师记》记载，古代以色列各部曾一度形成松散的联盟，在遇到危机时就设立一位士师作为领袖。士师是一个既非选举产生，也非世袭继承的职位。《圣经》把士师描写为被上帝选中来拯救以色列的人。士师平时掌管民事与诉讼，战时统领军队。在撒母耳膏立扫罗后，以色列历史上的士师时代结束。

以色列人的后代受到米甸人的侵扰①。基甸率一小队人马向米甸人发起进攻，并在神的干预下取得了胜利。以色列人欢欣鼓舞，将之归功于基甸的军事才能，并提议立之为王，说："愿你和你的儿孙管理我们。"这实在是一个极大的诱惑，拱手送给基甸的不但是一个王国，而且是世袭的。但是，基甸以虔诚之心回答道："我不管理你们，我的儿子也不管理你们。**唯有耶和华管理你们。**"没有比这更清楚明了的话了。基甸并不是拒绝荣誉，而是认为以色列人无权将这种荣誉授予他；他也没有用虚伪的感谢恭维以色列人，而是用先知的眼光，明确指斥他们背叛了自己真正的主人——上帝。

此后大概 130 年，以色列人又犯了同样的错误。他们对异教徒偶像崇拜风俗的向往简直令人不可理解。这一次，他们抓住了负责处理世俗事务的撒母耳两子的不端行为，突然发难，到撒母耳面前吵闹说："你年纪老迈了，你儿子不行你的道，现在请为我们立一个王治理我们，像列国一样。"②在此，我们不得不说他们动机不良，因为他们希望像其他民族那样，即像异教徒一样，

① 据《圣经》，米甸人是亚伯拉罕与妻子基土拉所生之子米甸的后代，是与古代以色列人关系密切的游牧部落。其活动范围大致在阿拉伯旷野西北部亚喀巴湾以东。米甸人以畜牧、行商和劫掠为生，在公元前 13 世纪—公元前 11 世纪期间，与以色列人冲突不断。

② 撒母耳年老时，立自己的两个儿子为士师。但两个儿子不信他的道，贪赃枉法，以致以色列众长老聚集起来，要求立王治理。于是，撒母耳就膏立扫罗为王。

但他们的真正荣耀却在于尽可能地与其他民族不同。当他们对撒母耳说"现在请为我们立一个王治理我们"时，撒母耳非常不快，于是向上帝祈祷。上帝告诉撒母耳："百姓向你说的一切话，你只管依从，因为他们不是厌弃你，而是厌弃我，**不要我作他们的王**。自从我领他们出埃及到如今，他们常常离开我，侍奉别神，现在他们向你所行的，是照他们素来所行的。故此你要依从他们的话，只是当警戒他们，告诉他们将来那王怎样管辖他们。"以色列人急于模仿的，不是某个国王的施政措施，而是世间所有国王的普遍做法。尽管古今异时，具体措施也大相径庭，但君主制的实质却从未改变。

撒母耳将上帝的话转告给那些要求他立王的人："管辖你们的王必这样行，他必派你们的儿子为他赶车，跟马，奔走在车前（这种描述与现在强行抓丁服役的情况毫无二致）。又必派他们作千夫长、五十夫长，为他耕种田地，收割庄稼，打造兵器和车上的器械。必取你们的女儿为他制造香膏，做饭烤饼（这段文字描写了国王的穷奢极欲和对百姓的压榨）。也必取你们最好的田地、葡萄园、橄榄园，赐给他的臣仆。你们的粮食和葡萄园所出的，也必取十分之一，给他的大臣和仆人（由此我们可以看到，行贿受贿、贪污腐败、徇私偏袒是国王们的顽疾）。又必取你们十分之一的仆人婢女、健壮的少年人和你们的驴，供他的差役。你们的羊群他必取十分之一，你们也必作他的仆人。

那时你们必因所选的王哀求耶和华，**耶和华却不应允你们。**"这段话解释了君主制绵延存续的原因。自古及今，圣君贤王寥寥无几，他们的品行既没有使国王的头衔变得神圣，也没有抹去国王的原罪。尽管《圣经》对大卫①称颂有加，但却对其国王身份毫不在意，只是强调他是一个讨得上帝欢心的人。但是，以色列人却拒绝执行撒母耳的训谕。他们说："不然，我们定要一个王治理我们，使我们像列国一样，有王治理我们，统领我们，为我们争战。"撒母耳继续劝说，但是徒劳无功。他甚至明确指出，他们这是对上帝忘恩负义，但还是没有任何效果。撒母耳看到人们执迷不悟，无奈喊道："我求告耶和华，他必打雷降雨（时值麦收时节，雷雨是一种不合农时的惩罚），使你们又知道又看出，**你们求立王的事，**是在耶和华面前犯大罪了。"于是，撒母耳向上帝祷告。上帝在这天降下大雷雨。见此情景，以色列人对上帝和撒母耳大为惧怕。他们对撒母耳说："求你为仆人们祷告耶和华你的神，免得我们死亡，**因为我们求立王的事，正是罪上加罪了。**"《圣经》的这部分内容措辞明确而肯定，

---

① 大卫，公元前 10 世纪以色列的第二任国王，这个名字的意思是"被爱的"。在《圣经》中，获得上帝眷顾的牧羊童大卫击杀了入侵以色列的非利士人的勇士歌利亚，而成为举国赞誉的少年英雄。他在登上王位后，通过一系列战争向四方扩张，建立了一个空前辽阔的以色列王国，开创了一个绵延数百年的王朝，因而被誉为以色列最伟大的国王和民族英雄。大卫的宗教地位极高，是"紧排在上帝的独生子之后的那个人"。

不容任何模棱两可的解读。

上帝确确实实在此表示反对君主制；如若不然，《圣经》就是伪书了。显然，在天主教国家里，国王、贵族和教士都竭尽全力不让民众看到这些经文，因为君主制政体毫无例外就是天主教会在世俗世界的翻版。

除了君主制的罪恶之外，这世上还有世袭继承这个弊害。前者是人类的自我堕落和自轻自贱；后者——据称是一种权利——则是对我们后代子孙的侮辱和欺骗。因为人人生而平等，所以没有人生来就有权给予自己的家族超越其他家族的永久优先权——尽管他本人或许应该获得同代人的高度赞誉，但他的后代可能根本不配继承这些荣光。证明王位世袭权荒唐愚蠢的最有力的自然证据就是，天道并不赞同这种制度。否则上天就不会经常把笨驴而不是雄狮赐给人类，从而使该制度沦为笑柄了。

人们起初只能拥有自己所获得的社会荣誉，因此，荣誉的授予者也无权出让子孙的权力。人们可以说："我们选你作我们的领袖"，但是他们却不能说："你的子孙和子孙的子孙将永远统治我们的后代"——这显然对他们自己的后代有失公允，因为这样一个愚蠢的、不公正的、违反常理的约定可能使他们在下一个国王即位后，处在一个恶棍或傻瓜的统治之下。就个人情感而言，大多数贤明之士曾经非常鄙视世袭权利；但是，这种权利也是一种一经确立就很难祛除的罪恶。许多人因恐惧而屈从；另一些人因迷信而盲从；那些更有权势的人则与国王瓜分从其他人那里掠夺来的赃物。

大家一般认为，当今世界上的王室都出身高贵。但是，很有可能，当我们揭开古老的黑色幕帘，追根溯源，就会发现，他们的始祖不过是某伙不法之徒的残暴的头子。其惨绝人寰的手段和阴险狡诈为他在这伙毛贼中赢得了首领的名号。通过扩充势力、升级劫掠活动，他震慑住了手无寸铁的温顺百姓，迫使他们经常进贡来换取自身的安全。但是，那些推举他作首领的人却不会打算把世袭的权利交给他的后代，因为这样一种将他们自己排除在外的做法与他们声称的一贯秉持的自由、自在的原则背道而驰。因此，在君主制初期，世袭继承并不是势在必行的，而是偶然的或补充性措施。但是，由于那个时代几乎没有，或者说根本没有记录留存下来，口耳相传的历史中又充斥着种种神话传说，因此，隔了几代之后，就很容易编造出一些迷信故事，假以时机，就像穆罕默德的故事那样，将世袭权利的概念硬生生地塞进民众的头脑之中。很有可能，在旧首领去世、新首领待选之时出现的令人惶惶不安，或者说似乎令人恐慌的混乱（暴徒中的选举不可能有条不紊）促使许多人支持世袭的主张。于是，世袭继承便堂而皇之地走上了前台。正像后来的历史那样，起初的变通之策后来竟成为一种言之凿凿的权利。

自从诺曼征服①以来，英国曾经有过那么几个贤明之君。但是，英伦大地更多的时候是在昏暴之君的统治下呻吟、流泪。但凡头脑清醒的人都不会说，他们在征服者威廉治下获得的权利是体面的。一个法国无赖带着一帮武装匪徒登陆，违背当地人民的意愿，自立为英格兰国王——简而言之，这个王朝肇始于一个卑鄙无耻的起点，其中没有任何神圣的因素。但是，如果有人愚蠢到竟然相信世袭权利，我们也没有必要花费大量时间去揭露世袭制的荒唐，就让他们浑浑噩噩、不加辨别地对驴子和狮子一并膜拜吧。我既不会模仿他们的谦卑，也不会妨碍他们的虔诚。

　　不过，我倒很乐意问问，这些人觉得国王最初是如何产生的？这个问题只可能有三个答案，即，或是通过抽签，或是通过选举，或是通过篡夺。

　　如果第一个国王是由抽签产生的，这就确立了一个排除了世袭继承的先例。扫罗②便是通过抽签被立为王的，他之后也未采用世袭继承，而且就传承顺序来看，其中也没有任何采用世袭制

---

　　① 1066 年 1 月，英王爱德华去世。9 月，法国诺曼底公爵威廉借口爱德华生前曾许其继承英国王位，率军渡海侵入英国。取得战争胜利之后，威廉于 12 月自立为英王，史称诺曼征服。威廉也因此被称为"征服者威廉"。

　　② 据《圣经》记载，扫罗是撒母耳遵照耶和华旨意膏立的以色列的第一位国王。但是，由于扫罗后来不遵行耶和华的旨意，耶和华后悔并"厌弃扫罗作以色列的王"。于是，撒母耳就按照耶和华的旨意又膏立大卫为王。

的意图。如果一个国家的第一位国王是由选举产生，也同样为后世树立了典范。要是说，由于第一批选民不仅选出了一位国王，还选出了一个世袭罔替的王族，从而剥夺了所有后世子孙的权利，那么，除了认定人类的自由意志断送于亚当之手的原罪说①外，《圣经》里里外外再也找不到任何类似的事例了。两相对照，显而易见，世袭继承的起源毫无荣耀可言。亚当体现了人类的原罪，第一批选民展示了人类的服从。在亚当那里，人类受到撒旦的驱使；而在第一批选民那里，人类屈服于君主的权威。前者使我们丧失了纯真，后者使我们丧失了权力。这一切导致我们无法再获得原先的某些地位与权利。毋庸置疑，原罪与世袭继承如出一辙。多么可耻的相提并论！多么丢脸的联系！就是最巧舌如簧的诡辩家也无法想出比这更贴切的比喻了。

还没有人大胆到为篡位辩护。而征服者威廉就是一个篡位者，这一事实不容辩驳。事实上，英国君主政体的历史是经不起推敲的。

但是，对人类而言，世袭继承的罪恶远比其荒谬严重得多。如果世袭制能确保贤德之人得居正位，则就有了神权的支持与证

---

① 原罪说是基督教的重要教义之一。据《圣经》，人类的始祖亚当和夏娃生活在伊甸园中，因受了蛇的诱惑，违背上帝的命令偷吃禁果，"亏欠了上帝的荣耀"。这罪遗传给后世子孙，成为人类一切罪恶、灾难、痛苦和死亡的根源。人一生下来，在上帝面前就是一个"罪人"，所以需要被救赎。

明。但是，由于它给蠢货、坏蛋、违法乱纪者打开了一扇大门，它便包含了某种压迫性。那些自认为天生就是统治者的人，往往迅速变得粗野无礼。因为他们觉得自己是从芸芸众生中挑选出来的，心灵早早就被傲慢侵蚀殆尽。他们生活的世界与大多数人的世界有极大的不同，以致他们几乎没有机会去了解这个世界的真正利益所在。当他们继承王位的时候，往往是整个国家中最无知、最不称职的人。

世袭继承的另一个恶果就是，会出现幼主登基的情况。此时，摄政之人以国王为幌子，有种种机会、面对各种诱惑去背叛信任。当国王年迈体衰，进入人生最后阶段的时候，国家也会祸端频起。在上述两种情况下，恶棍人渣们会成功地操控年老昏聩或年幼无知的君主，而百姓则沦为他们的牺牲品。

在所有支持世袭继承的理由中，貌似最有道理的一条是：它使国家免于内战。如果真是这样，倒不失为一个举足轻重的理由。但事实上，这却是强加给人类的最恬不知耻的谎言。整个英国历史都否认了这一观点。自从诺曼征服以来，共有30个国王和两个幼主统治过这个混乱不堪的国家。在此期间，至少爆发了8次内战和19次叛乱（包括光荣革命）。可见，世袭继承并没有带来和平，反而不利于和平，并摧毁了和平似乎赖以存在的基础。

在兰开斯特家族和约克家族之间爆发的英格兰王位继承战

争①，使英国在数年中烽烟四起，血流成河。除了小规模的冲突和战斗之外，兰开斯特家族的亨利与约克家族的爱德华之间还进行过 12 场激战。亨利两次被爱德华俘虏，而后者也曾沦为前者的阶下囚。当争端仅仅起于私事的时候，战事就反复无常，民意则微妙难料。亨利得意洋洋地被人从监狱送进王宫，而爱德华则被迫流亡国外；转瞬之间，亨利又被逐下王位，爱德华则被召回即位。而议会总是追随得胜的一方。

玫瑰战争始于亨利六世②时代，直至亨利七世③统一了两个王族，仍未结束，即从 1422 年延续至 1489 年，长达 67 年。

简而言之，君主制与世袭继承使整个世界（并不仅仅是这个或那个王国）毁于血泊与灰烬之中。这是一种上帝明确出言反对的政体，流血漂橹的场景与它如影随形。

如果我们仔细探究国王的职守，就会发现（在某些国家里，国王根本无事可做），他们饱食终日，既没有自己的人生乐趣，

---

① 英格兰王位继承战争史称玫瑰战争（一般认为起止时间为 1455—1485 年，但存在不同的看法。本书作者就认为，战争起止时间为 1422—1489 年），是两个贵族家族为争夺英格兰王位而进行的内战。战争双方兰开斯特家族和约克家族都是英王爱德华三世的后裔，族徽分别是红玫瑰、白玫瑰，"玫瑰战争"即由此得名。1485 年，代表兰开斯特家族的亨利·都铎率军取胜，夺得王位，是为亨利七世。然后，他娶了约克家族的继承人伊丽莎白为妻，使两个家族联合起来。

② 亨利六世（1421—1471），英国国王，1422—1461 年、1470—1471 年在位。

③ 亨利七世（1457—1509），英国国王，1485—1507 年在位。

也无益于国家，然后退出历史舞台，让继任者重复无所事事的人生旅程。在君主专制政体中，民事和军事大权都系于国王一身。以色列人的子孙在请求立王时，恳求说："有王治理我们，统领我们，为我们争战。"但是，在英国这样的国家里，国王既不是法官，也不是将军，人们不禁困惑不解，国王是干什么的？

越接近共和制的政体，国王承担的职责就越少。要想给英国政体找到一个合适的名字，还真有点困难。威廉·梅瑞迪斯爵士①称之为共和国。但就其现状而言，它实在不配有此称呼。因为王权的腐朽势力通过随意支配各方面事务吞噬了全部权力，并抵消、耗尽了下议院（政体中的共和制部分）的积极作用。所以，跟法国和西班牙差不多，英国政体基本上就是君主制。

人们往往尚未理解其含义就因名谓而发生争执。其实，英国人深感自豪的并不是英国政体中的君主制部分，而是共和制部分，即从自己内部选出下议院议员的自由。而且，显而易见，当共和政体的效力衰退的时候，奴役就接踵而来。唉，英国政体之所以病入膏肓，不就是因为君主制毒害了共和制，王权控制了下议院？

在英国，国王能做的也就是挑起战争、封官赐爵这些陷国

---

① 威廉·梅瑞迪斯（1725?—1790），18世纪晚期英国政治家，罗金汉辉格党人。

家于赤贫和纷争之中的事。如果一个人一年收入 80 万英镑，还受人尊敬，那确实是个不错的买卖。一个诚实的普通人对于社会的价值及其在上帝眼中的价值，远远高于自古至今所有戴王冠的无赖。

第三章　对当前北美形势的看法

没有差别就不会导致地位出现高下之分；彻底的平等就不会产生诱惑。

在下文中，我将仅仅陈述不加修饰的事实、显而易见的观点和常识。我对读者别无他求，只希望你们能摒弃成见和先入之见，让理性和情感做主，并且保持或不丢掉自己的真实个性，超越时代局限地丰富、扩大眼界。

关于英国和北美殖民地之间的斗争的书籍已经汗牛充栋。各色人等出于各种动机和不同的目的参与论战，但一切都是徒劳。现在，论辩结束了。英王挑起了战争，而北美大陆接受了挑战。武力成为决定胜负的最终手段。

据说，已故的佩勒姆先生①（他是一个颇有才干的大臣，但

----

① 亨利·佩勒姆（1694—1754），英国辉格党政治家，1743—1754年任首相兼财政大臣。在他任职期间，英国国内局势稳定；其财政政策获得很高的赞誉。

并非毫无错误）由于其措施的临时性而遭到下议院抨击时，回答说："它们将在我执政的时间里推行。"如果殖民地人民在当前的斗争中秉持这样一种致命的、怯懦的想法，我们的后代将会满心憎恶地想起祖先的名字。

太阳从未照耀过比这场斗争更有价值的事业。这不是一个城市、一个地区、一个省份，或一个王国的事，而是一个大陆的事——一块至少占地球可居面积八分之一的大陆；这不是关系一天、一年，或一个时代的事，事实上，我们的子孙后代都被卷入其中，并将永远或多或少地受到当前行动的影响。现在是在北美大陆播种团结、忠诚和荣誉等信念的时刻。今天留下的最微小的痕迹，都将像是用针尖在小橡树柔嫩的树皮上刻下的名字——它会随着树木的生长而扩大，子孙后代将看到几个醒目的大字。

当处理问题的手段从争论变为武力，一个新的政治领域便出现了，一种新的思维方式也产生了。4 月 19 日之前，也就是战争开始①之前所提出的所有计划、议案等都已成为明日黄花。尽管它们在当时是适当之策，但现在已彻底作废，毫无用处了。

---

① 1775 年 4 月 19 日，在莱克星敦打响了美国独立战争的第一枪，史称"莱克星敦的枪声"，这一事件揭开了美国独立战争的序幕。1775 年 4 月 18 日，马萨诸塞总督根据密报，派遣英军前往康科德（在波士顿附近），搜缴当地民兵的秘密军火库。消息被北美民兵截获。4 月 19 日，当英军进至莱克星敦一带时，与民兵交火，民兵有多人伤亡。英军在返程途中，再次受到北美人的偷袭，伤亡不小。此后，英王发布告谕，宣布北美殖民地的反抗为非法，声言"宁可丢掉王冠，决不放弃战争"。随后，英国议会通过了派遣军队赴北美镇压的决议。

无论就这一问题论辩双方有多大分歧，他们最终殊途同归，一致认为，应同英国联合。双方唯一的差别在于，达到目的的手段不同。一方诉诸武力，而另一方寄希望于友谊。不过，到目前为止，实际情况是，前者已然失败，后者的影响也不复存在。

　　与英国和解的好处曾被连篇累牍地大肆渲染，但它就像一场转瞬即逝的黄粱美梦，最终只留下我们在原地踏步。所以，不妨考虑一下另外一方的独立主张，探究、估算北美殖民地与英国保持联系并依附于英国所要承受的，并将一直承受的重大损害。我们应根据天道公理和常识来检查审视这种联系和依附，认真考量，如果独立，我们必须依靠什么；如果依附，我们可以抱有什么希望。

　　我听说，有人断言，因为北美曾经在英国的庇护下繁荣昌盛，所以，保持与英国的联系对北美未来的福祉就是必不可少、永不可缺的。再没有比这更荒谬的观点了！你还不如说，既然小孩因喝牛奶而茁壮成长，他就应该永远不吃肉；或者说，我们人生的头 20 年将是下一个 20 年的模板。这是十足的强词夺理。我不妨直截了当地点明，即便没有欧洲强国参与其中，北美照样会欣欣向荣，甚至可能更加强盛。北美因出口贸易而繁盛，其外销物资均为生活必需品，只要欧洲人还吃饭，就不会没有销路。

　　有人说，英国曾经保护过我们。没错，英国确实曾经独占北美，并且花着我们的和它自己的钱保护北美。不过，出于商业和政治的考虑，它同样也会保护土耳其。

唉！长期以来，我们被过时的偏见引入歧途，为迷信做出巨大的牺牲。我们曾因受到英国的保护而自得，却从没有想过，它的动机是其自身的利益，而不是英美之间的情谊。英国出手相救并不是为了我们，并不是保护我们免受我们的敌人的侵略；而是出于其自身的考虑，抗击它自己的敌人；并与那些原本和我们没有任何纷争，却因英国与我们彻底决裂的人为敌。如若英国人不放弃他们声称在北美所享有的权利，北美大陆自将摆脱他们的控制。这样一来，如果法国、西班牙与英国交战，我们仍可与它们保持和平友好。此前，汉诺威王朝战争带来的灾难警示我们，不要再保持与英国的关系了。

最近，国会里有人声称，北美各殖民地只有通过母邦英国才彼此关联。也就是说，宾夕法尼亚、新泽西以及其他殖民地都是经由英国才联系在一起的。这确实是拐弯抹角地证明彼此相关的方法，但也是最便捷且唯一真实地证明双方存在敌意的方法——如果我可以这么说的话。法国和西班牙从来都不是，将来也永远不会是北美人的敌人，但他们是英国臣民的敌人。

有人断言，英国是北美的母邦。如果确实如此，英国的行为就更加可耻了。虎毒尚且不食子，连未开化的野蛮人都不会与自己的亲族开战。因此，指认英国为母邦，反倒是对英国的谴责。事实上，这种观点是错误的，顶多也不过是部分正确。

英王及其附庸居心叵测地使用的"宗主国"或"母邦"这个词儿，其实出于卑鄙的天主教目的，妄图利用我们轻信的弱点，从有失公允的偏见中获利。整个欧洲，而不单单是英国，才是北美的母邦。北美新世界曾是欧洲各地饱受迫害的、热爱公民自由和宗教自由的人士的避难所。他们逃亡到此，并不是为了离开母亲温柔的怀抱，而是为了躲避惨无人道的暴行。曾将第一批移民逐出家园的残暴统治仍在追逐他们的子孙。迄今为止，英国的情况仍然如此。

在北美这片广袤的土地上，我们淡忘了360英里的狭小局促（英国的范围），更大范围地传播我们的友谊。我们声称与每一个欧洲基督徒都亲如兄弟，并为这种慷慨大度而自豪。

随着对世界了解的加深、扩大，我们会逐步克服地方偏见。观察这个过程，是一件令人高兴的事。出生在任何一个以教区为基本单位的英国城镇的人，自然与本教区的教友关系最密切（因为在很多情况下，他们的利益都是一致的），并互称"街坊"；如果两个"街坊"在离家区区几英里之外相遇，就会摒弃街巷的狭隘观念，以"乡亲"相称；如果远游于郡外时相遇，就会忘记里巷、城镇这种狭隘分类，而径称"同乡"，即同郡人；如果游历异邦，在法国或其他任何欧洲国家相遇，他们的地方意识就会扩大成为"英国人"这个概念。同样道理，欧洲人在北美或世界任何一个角落相遇，都是同胞。因为就全世界而言，无论是英国、荷兰、德国，还是瑞典在较大范围的区划层级内所处的位置，与街道、城镇、郡在较小范围的区划层级内的位置是一样的。对于北美民众来说，这些分类法太狭隘了。即便在本州（宾夕法尼亚）的居民中，英国人的后裔也不到三分之一。因此，我质疑单单把"宗主国"或"母邦"这个词用在英国身上的行为——这是错误、自私、狭隘、不公的。

即便我们都承认自己是英国人的后裔，又有什么意义？完全没有！既然现在英国已是我们公开的敌人，它就被剥夺了所有其他名字和头衔。那种认为和解是我们的责任的说法真是滑稽透顶。当今英国王室的第一个国王（征服者威廉）是个法国人，而且半数英国贵族也都是法国人的后裔。那么，同理而言，英国就应该被法国统治了。

已有卷帙浩繁的文字讨论过英国与北美殖民地联合起来可能产生的力量。据说，二者携手即可傲视寰宇。但是，这只不过是个猜想。既然战争的胜负难以预料，这句话也就毫无意义了。反正北美大陆绝不会耗尽自己的人力去支持英国在亚洲、非洲或欧洲的军事行动。

此外，挑战全世界与北美有什么关系？我们的计划是发展贸易。如果按既定方针悉心经营，我们将赢得整个欧洲的和平与友谊，因为把北美打造成为一个自由贸易港，是全欧洲的利益所在。北美的贸易地位就是对自身的保护，而北美又会因为匮乏金银资源而免遭入侵。

　　我对和解方案最狂热的支持者提出质疑，要求他们列举北美联合英国可能获得的好处，哪怕一个也行。我一再追问，但是连一个好处也没有。我们的谷物将在欧洲市场上按价出售，我们的进口货物一定在我们愿意购买的地方成交。

　　与此同时，与英国联合给北美带来的伤害和不利却不可胜数。我们对全人类的及对自己的责任都要求我们切断这种关系。对英国的任何屈从或依赖，都会直接导致北美大陆深陷于欧洲战争与争斗之中，使我们与一些国家产生摩擦。这些国家本来打算与我们和平共处；而我们与它们既无宿怨，也无过节。既然欧洲是我们的商品市场，我们就应该对各国一视同仁，不偏不倚。远离欧洲纷争才是北美的真正利益所在。如果依附于英国，北美就被挟持成为英国政治天平上的一个砝码，断然不可能置身事外。

　　欧洲大陆王国众多，不可能长期保持和平。无论何时，只要英国与其他国家开战，北美的贸易就会因其与英国的关系而毁于一旦。下一场战争也许与之前的不同，但如果情况未如所料，现在主张和解的人，到时就会希望独立了。因为在那种情况下，中立更安全。所有正确的、合理的事都在呼吁摆脱英国的控制。被屠杀者的鲜血和造化的悲啼发出呼喊："是分手的时候了。"甚至全知全能的上帝在英国和北美之间设置的距离，也是一个支持北美独立的扎实有力、合情合理的证据。它说明，英国凌驾于北美之上绝不是上帝的安排。而发现北美大陆的时间以及移民的方式，更加坐实了这一看法。宗教改革之后不久，美洲便被发现了。这仿佛是上帝仁慈的施予，特意为后来在故土既得不到友谊，也没有安全保障的受迫害者开辟了一个避难所。

　　大不列颠对北美的管辖权是一种迟早必将终结的统治形式。一个认真的人会痛苦地意识到，他口中的"现在这个统治形式"只是一种临时性的存在。在这种情形下展望未来，他绝不会感到真正的快乐。身为父母，知道这个政府岌岌可危，无法为我们遗留给后代的任何东西提供保障，我们会快快不乐。简而言之，我们不应让下一代子孙背负我们的欠债，而应自己承担起来。否则，我们对后代就太无耻、太卑鄙了。为了正确界定自己的职责，我们应该照顾我们的孩子，确定自己的位置并随着时间的推移而逐渐提升。当我们达到一定高度的时候，就会看到被现在的恐惧和偏见所遮蔽的前景。

　　尽管我小心翼翼地避免不必要的冒犯，但是我不得不直言不讳地说明，我认为，所有赞成和解的人都可以被归为以下几种类型：利欲熏心，不堪信任的人；意志薄弱，没有眼光的人；固执己见，不愿正视现实的人；还有一批态度温和，但对欧洲世界评价过高的人。相比前三者，最后一类由于判断失误、考虑欠妥，将会给北美大陆带来更多的灾难。

对于许多人来说，远离灾难现场确实是一件幸事。厄运还没有不偏不倚地落在他们头上，所以他们并不觉得整个北美殖民地的财富都危如累卵。那么，让我们的想象暂时带我们去趟波士顿吧。这个多灾多难的地方将令我们清醒，并且警示我们，要与不可信任的政权永远断绝关系。这个不幸的城市的居民在几个月前还过着安逸而富足的日子，现在却除了留在当地挨饿，或外出乞讨之外，别无选择①。如果继续留在城里，他们可能被自己人的炮火所伤；如果出城逃命，可能遭到军队的洗劫。他们目前的处境就像毫无获救希望的囚徒。甚至在发动总攻去营救他们的时候，他们也会因此而暴露在双方的连天炮火之下。

　　性格消极的人多少有点轻率地原谅了英国对我们的伤害。他们怀抱乐观的希望，动不动就高呼："来吧，尽管发生了这一切，让我们再次成为朋友吧。"但是，想想人类的情感和感觉吧。用自然伦理这个试金石来检验一下和解的主张，然后告诉我，你们将来是否能够热爱、尊敬并忠心服务于那个在你们的土地上烧杀抢掠的政权？如果做不到，那你们就是在自欺欺人，

---

　　① 指波士顿之围。1775 年 4 月 19 日—1776 年 3 月 17 日的波士顿之围是北美独立战争开始阶段的重大事件。1775 年 4 月，北美殖民地的新英格兰民兵（后成为大陆军的一部分）包围了马萨诸塞的波士顿城，阻止城内的英军调动，切断了英国海军的作战补给。英军试图突围，但未获成功。随后，大陆会议决定建立大陆军，并选举乔治·华盛顿为总司令。1776 年 3 月，华盛顿将重炮布置在波士顿外的制高点上，英军指挥官意识到再也无法固守此城，只得撤离。

而且，你们造成的延误将给后代子孙带来灭顶之灾。你们既不热爱英国，也不尊敬她。那么，你们将来与英国建立的联系，就是被迫的、不正常的，只是暂时的权宜之计。英美关系很快就会回到老路上，甚至比原先更糟糕。如果你们说，你们能对这些暴行泰然处之。那么，你们的房子可曾被焚毁？你们的财产可曾在你的面前被破坏？你们的妻儿可有床安卧，有食果腹？你们的父母儿女是否落入他们之手，而你们自己则是堕落颓废、悲惨可怜的幸存者？如果你们统统没有经历过这些，那就无权评判那些历尽浩劫的人。如果你们曾经历一切磨难，却仍然能与施暴者握手言欢，那就不配被称为丈夫、父亲、朋友或爱人。无论你们这一辈子将获得什么样的地位或头衔，你们都有一颗怯懦的心和一个势利的魂。

这不是煽风点火，也不是夸大其词，而是用符合天道人伦的正常感觉和情感来分析问题。如果没有这些感觉和情感，我们就不能履行社会职责，或者无法享受人生乐趣。我并不是渲染惨状，挑起仇恨，而是想把大家从致命而怯懦的麻木不仁中唤醒，去坚定地追求既定的目标。北美只会因自己的拖拖拉拉、胆小怯懦而沦丧。除此之外，无论是英国，还是其他欧洲列强都无法征服这片大陆。如果使用得当，眼下这个冬季将发挥决定性作用，成为历史的转折；但是，如果我们虚掷光阴或掉以轻心，整个北美大陆将陷入万劫不复。倘若有人浪费了这段珍贵而有用的时光，无论他是谁、担任何职、身在何方，任何惩罚对他来说都是罪有应得。

那种认为北美大陆可以更长期地屈从于外部势力的看法是不理性的，是违反宇宙秩序的，也是违背历史事实的。甚至最乐观的英国人也不这样想。现在，人类最智慧的头脑也无法设计出一个既不独立，又能给北美大陆提供哪怕一年安全的方案。和解只是一个虚妄的梦。造化已然放弃了这个选择，人力无法增益。正像弥尔顿睿智的表述："不解的冤仇创伤深似海，真诚的和解难如愿。"①

各种温和地争取和平的方法都失效了。我们的请愿均被不屑一顾地驳回。这使我们确信，没有什么比反复请愿更能满足国王的虚荣心、坐实他们的固执。也正是这种行为造就了欧洲国王的专制，看看丹麦和瑞典吧！既然只有反抗才有用，那么，看在上帝的份上，让我们实现最终的独立，不要让我们的后代在被肆意篡改的、毫无意义的母邦—属国的名义下惨遭毒手。

认为英国人再也不会压榨北美的观点，是毫无意义的空想。

---

① 约翰·弥尔顿（1608—1674），英国诗人、政论家，出生于清教徒家庭，一生追求资产阶级民主。他的代表作、长篇史诗《失乐园》取材于《圣经》中的创世纪故事，表达了诗人对自由的强烈渴望，是西方文学史上的不朽之作。引文出自《失乐园》第四卷。该卷讲述了撒旦在反抗上帝失败后，为了复仇，潜入伊甸园，引诱亚当、夏娃偷吃上帝明令禁吃的果子的故事。

我们曾对取消《印花税法案》①抱有同样的幻想，但是，短短一两年的时间，包括我在内，所有人的迷梦都被打碎了。如果上述看法是正确的，我们也可以据此推定，那些曾被击败的国家绝不会再次挑起争端。

说到管理，英国根本无法公正合理地处理北美大陆的事务。殖民地的事务很快就会变得繁杂无比。一个与我们天各一方，对我们一无所知的国家无法用权宜之计解决种种问题。如果英国人不能征服我们，他们也不能管理我们。为了流言蜚语或陈情诉状而奔波三四千英里，等待四五个月才有答复，然后再等五六个月来对之进行解释。不出几年，这就会被看作是愚蠢、幼稚之举。假如这曾经一度是适当之举，那么也应有一个适当的时机终止它。

没有自卫能力的小岛是国王们觊觎的合适目标。但是，倘若认为一个大陆将会被一个岛国永远统治下去，则是荒谬至极。自然界从来没有卫星大于主星的例子。既然英国和北美的关系违反了正常的自然秩序，显而易见，它们各自独立，分属不同的系统：英国属于欧洲，而北美属于它自己。

---

① 1765 年，英国首相乔治·格伦威尔通过了《印花税法案》(Stamp Act)，要求北美殖民地的印刷品，如报纸、小册子、遗嘱、历书、执照、商业契约等都要交纳 1 分至 50 元不等的印花税。这种明目张胆的经济压榨引起了北美殖民地的强烈不满，它们开始采取统一的行动反抗英国的统治。北美殖民地还向英国议会递交了一份正式抗议。1776 年，英国议会虽然迫于压力废除了《印花税法案》，但却在同一天通过了一部新法案，声明"无论是在何种事务上"，英国议会都对北美殖民地拥有合法的权力。

我并不是因为自尊、党派之争或仇恨而主张英美分离、北美独立的。我清楚明确、发自内心地坚信，这是北美大陆的真正利益所在。不独立，任何行动都只是拆东墙补西墙，无法带来长久的幸福——这不但使我们的子孙面临杀戮，而且是在咬咬牙、使使劲就能给北美大陆带来莫大荣耀的关键时刻临阵退缩。

既然英国丝毫没有表示出和解的意向，我们可以确信，双方无法达成北美能够接受的协议，或者说，任何方式都无法补偿我们已经损失的生命和财富。

我们的奋斗目标应该与付出的代价相称。诺斯的辞职，或者说那个可恶的小集团的垮台①，根本不值得我们花费数百万元。如果那些令我们怨声载道的法案都能撤销的话，暂时的贸易中断尽管有所不便，但还是值得付出的代价。不过，倘若整个大陆都必须拿起武器，每个人都必须成为战士，仅仅反对一个可鄙的政府部门就不值得了。假如我们的斗争目标就是为了废除那些法案，代价就太高昂了。平心静气地估算一下，无论是为了捍卫法律，还是为了夺取土地，付出邦克山战役②这样的代价都是愚不可及

---

① 1763 年 5 月，乔治·格伦威尔出任英国首相。由于对《印花税法案》处理不力等原因，他于 1765 年 7 月下台，时任财政大臣的弗雷德里克·诺斯也随之辞职。

② 邦克山是位于波士顿附近查尔斯顿的一座山丘。1775 年 6 月 17 日，发生在此地的邦克山战役是美国独立战争早期的著名战役之一，也是"波士顿之围"（1775 年 4 月—1776 年 3 月）的组成部分。此役，英军虽然获胜，但伤亡惨重，收获甚微，仅仅攻占了邦克山，仍旧无法解除北美民兵对波士顿的围困。邦克山战役之名后来在西方被作为得不偿失的代名词。

的。我一向坚信，北美大陆迟早必然独立。从最近北美快速发展成熟的情况来看，独立近在咫尺。既然战争已经爆发，我们就不必再为此发生口舌之争，时间将最终解决一切问题。非要纠缠于此，那就像是控告一个租约刚刚到期的房客非法侵占一样，纯属画蛇添足。在1775年4月19日那个灾难的日子（莱克星敦屠杀）之前，我比任何人都更热衷于和解。但是，当惨剧被公诸天下时，我便与那个心冷如铁、暴戾恣睢的英国法老永远决裂了。我鄙视这个恶棍。他伪称自己是万民之父，但却对子民被屠的消息无动于衷，灵魂沾染着他们的鲜血沉沉入梦。

如果认定事情已成定局，结果将会怎样？我的回答是，结果是北美大陆的毁灭。原因如下：

首先，统治权仍然在英王手中，他会否决北美大陆的所有立法。既然英王已经证明自己与自由势不两立并对专制权力痴迷思服，他难道不正是那个告诉北美殖民地"你们只能制定我喜欢的法律"的人吗？在北美的土地上，是否有人无知透顶，甚至不知道，根据现行体制，除非英王授权，北美大陆不能制定法律？是否有人糊涂至极，以致看不出（根据已发生的事实），除了那些符合英王意图的法律外，他不会让我们在这里制定任何法律？由于北美没有自己的法律，我们遵行的是英国为我们制定的法律，因此我们可能彻底地沦为奴隶。在解决事端之后（有人这么说），英王定会倾其所能，使北美大陆恭顺、谦服。这一点难道还有疑问吗？如果不勇往直前，我们只能或是退缩，或是纷争不止，或是可笑地请愿上书。我们的繁荣强大已远远超出了英王的期望，难道他将来不会想方设法地削弱我们吗？简而言之，一个对我们的繁荣昌盛心存嫉妒的政权，还适合统治我们吗？凡是对此答"不"的人，都是主张独立的人，因为独立意味着，是我们制定自己的法律，还是让北美大陆现在的和将来可能的最大的敌人——英王告诉我们"除了合我心意的，此处不得有任何法律"？

你可能会说，英王在英国也有否决权。不经他同意，英国人也不能制定法律。按照常理，一个21岁的小年轻（这是常有的事）对几百万民众——其中不乏比他更年长、更睿智者——说："我禁止你们提出的这项或那项法案成为法律"，这是极其荒唐的。尽管我绝不会停止揭露这种荒谬，但是，在现在的情况下，我的回答是："英国是英王的居所，而北美不是。二者的情况截然不同。"英王在北美拥有否决权的危害比在英国大十倍。因为，在英国，英王几乎不会否决一个意图加强英国国防的议案；但是在北美，英王绝不会让类似的议案通过。

在英国的政治体系中，北美不过是个二等成员。英国只有在实现自己意图的情况下，才会考虑北美的利益。因此，出于自身利益的考量，英国在那些不能给它带来好处的地方处处压制我们的发展，至少是设置障碍。就已发生的种种事件来看，在这样一个"二手政府"的统治下，我们很快就会"形势大好"！人们不会因为改名换姓就化敌为友。为了提醒大家，当下，和解是一种危险的论调，我必须指出，英王为了恢复对北美十三州的控制，会采取怀柔手段，废除那些激起民怨的法案。其目的只是妄图通过长期耍弄阴谋诡计而达到无法用武力在短期内实现的目标。对北美而言，和解与毁灭其实就是一个硬币的两面。

其次，我们所能期望得到的最优厚的条件，也只不过是权宜之计，或是一种被监管的政府。这种政府到殖民地发展成熟的时候就维持不下去了。因此，在过渡期里，总体事态和局面都是悬而未决、毫无希望的。有资产的移民不愿到一个政体悬于一线、整日徘徊于暴乱边缘的国家来。而大量的现有居民将抓紧时间处理产业，然后离开这片大陆。

在所有支持独立的理由中，最有力的一点就是，只有独立（即建立北美大陆自己的政府），才能维护北美和平，使之免于内战之火。我担心，现在一旦与英国和解，接踵而来的就是某处暴乱，其后果比英国的所有恶意还要严重得多。

成千上万的人已经被英国的暴行毁灭，更多的人可能面临着同样的厄运。那些人的想法与我们这些未经苦难的人不一样。他们为争取自由而献出了曾经拥有的一切，现在一无所有，仅剩自由。既然再也无甚可失，他们自然鄙视投降屈服。此外，北美殖民地对英国政府的态度就像是一个即将走出青春期的少年那样无所顾忌。一个不能维持和平稳定局面的政府就不成其为政府，供养这样的政府就是浪费金钱。如果在和解之后的第二天发生暴乱，而英国对北美的权力只是纸上谈兵，我们能祈望英国做什么呢？我曾经听到有些人说，他们之所以害怕独立，是因为担心这会导致内战。我相信，他们中的大部分人都是不假思索、脱口而出的。未经斟酌的想法基本上都是错误的，这次也不例外。靠修修补补勉强维持的关系比独立更加令人担心。我站在受害者的立场上声言，如果被驱离家园，产业被毁，境遇窘迫，作为一个有血性的汉子，我绝不会拥护和解的主张，也不会觉得自己对之负有任何责任和义务。

北美各殖民地已经展现出了良好的秩序和遵从大陆政府的精神。这足以使所有理智的人都对这个领导机构感到放心和满意。我们完全没有理由担心，一个殖民地将会想方设法凌驾于另一个殖民地之上。只有那些十足幼稚荒唐的理由，才会让人杞人忧天。

没有差别就不会导致地位出现高下之分；彻底的平等就不会产生诱惑。欧洲各共和国都（我们可以说总是）和平稳定。荷兰与瑞士，无论内外，均无战事。而君主制国家却从来没有享受过长期的和平安宁。从内来说，王位本身就是野心勃勃的暴徒们的觊觎对象；此外，与王权如影随形的狂妄、傲慢也会渐渐膨胀，最终引发国际争端。而在同样的情况下，建立在更自然的原则基础上的共和制政府却能纠正这个错误。

如果真有什么原因让我们为独立担心的话，那就是尚没有制定计划，人们看不到出路何在。因此，我愿奉献如下几点看法作为这项事业的开始。同时，我实实在在地承认，我提出这些意见，只是为了抛砖引玉。将各人的零散想法汇集起来，常常能形成某种素材，可供睿智者提炼发挥，化腐朽为神奇。

各殖民地会议应该每年召开一次，并且只设一个会议主席。代表们更加平等，他们的议题全部围绕内部事务展开，并且听命于大陆会议。

每个殖民地因地制宜地分为六、八或十个区。每个区都推举出适当数量的代表参加大陆会议，所以，每个殖民地至少有30名代表。而大陆会议的代表总数至少是390人。每一届大陆会议都应用如下方式召集并选出一个会议主席：当代表们齐聚一堂时，用抽签的办法从全部13个殖民地中挑出一个，然后让所有代表投票，在该殖民地代表中选出一人为会议主席。到下一届会议时，除去选出上届会议主席的那个殖民地外，从其余12个殖民地中抽签选出一个，再投票从中选出会议主席。依此类推，直到13个殖民地都轮上为止。为了保证所通过法律的公正性，3/5以上的人数才能被称为"多数"。在这样一个公平组织的政府中，任何挑拨离间者都是想加入撒旦反抗上帝行列的人。

既然这件事最初应由谁，或以什么方式启动颇为棘手；既然似乎最合适的办法就是让处于统治者和被统治者之间的中间团体，即居于大陆会议和人民二者之间的团体来做，那就让殖民地会议按如下方式，遵循如下宗旨召开吧：组成一个 26 人的大陆会议委员会，即每个殖民地有两个名额。由各州议会或制宪会议产生两名委员。从全州人民中选出 5 名代表并捍卫全州利益的人选。他们将由来自全州各地的、所有有资格的选民在州首府选举产生；为了方便起见，代表也可从各州人口最稠密的两三个地区产生。这种召集会议的方式将处理事务的两大原则——知识与权力——结合起来。大陆会议、各州议会或制宪会议的代表已有从政经验，他们将会成为能干而高效的公职人员。而上述机构的权力既然得自人民，那就具有确实合法的权威。

议员们应着手制定《大陆宪章》或称《联合殖民地宪章》（名称与所谓的英国《大宪章》相对应）；确定大陆会议、各州议会的代表人数、选举办法和会期，并且明确它们各自的职责和权力范围。我们要始终牢记，我们的力量来自于整个大陆，而不是单个殖民地。要在良心的指引下，捍卫所有人的自由和财产——尤其是宗教信仰的自由——以及其他类似的、有必要写入宪章的权利。此后，上述会议应立即解散，依据《宪章》选出的那些人将暂时担任北美大陆的立法者和管理者。愿上帝保佑他们的和平与幸福，阿门！

如果将来某些人因此或是类似的某个目的被选为代表，我愿把博学的政体观察者德拉戈内蒂①的话送给他们："政治家的科学在于确认幸福与自由的真实要义。那些创建了使国家以最小的花费，维护个人的最大幸福的政体的人，理应获得我们的世代感激。"

有人也许会问，北美的国王在哪里？朋友，我告诉你，他在天上统治着，不像英国国王那样涂炭生灵。即便就世俗荣誉而言，我们也不应觉得遗憾。让我们庄严地选定一天来公布《宪章》；让它以神圣的律法、上帝之言为依据；让我们给它加冕，从而告诉世界，如果说我们赞成君主政体，那么在北美，法律就是国王。在专制政体中，国王就是法律；同样的，在自由国家中，法律应该就是国王，除此无他。但是，为了避免以后出现滥用权力的情况，就让我们在庆典结束时取消国王这一称号，将其权力散给有权享受它的人民。

建立自己的政府是我们的天赋权利。如果认真考察人事的变幻无常，我们就会确信，理智冷静、深思熟虑地组建自己的政府并掌握权力远比把这件利益攸关的大事交付时运更明智，也更安全。倘若我们现在忽略此事，将来就可能再次出现一个马萨涅

---

① 德拉戈内蒂（1738—1818），意大利政治家。引文出自他的专著《论美德与报酬》。该书 1765 年出版于意大利那不勒斯，1769 年在伦敦出版了英译本，是当时欧美政治家、学者的必读之书。

罗①。他会操控民众的焦虑，并纠集亡命之徒和牢骚之辈篡夺政权，然后像秋风扫落叶那样将北美大陆的自由一扫而光。如果北美的政权再次落入英国人之手，动荡的局势会诱使某个孤注一掷的冒险家来碰碰运气。在这种情况下，英国能给我们什么帮助？它还没有耳闻，灾难事件即已发生。我们就会遭受征服者威廉治下的、可怜的不列颠人曾经历的那些苦难。你们这些反对独立的人，根本不知道自己在干什么。你们令政权出现真空，从而为绵绵不绝的暴政敞开了大门。

野蛮可憎的英国人曾经煽动印第安人和黑人来消灭我们。这种暴行背负着双重罪恶：既对我们残忍无情，又背叛出卖了印第安人和黑人。因此，千千万万人都坚信，将英国人驱逐出美洲大陆是无尚的光荣。我们的理智禁止我们相信某些人，而我们那已被伤害得千疮百孔的感情则命令我们去憎恨他们。与这样一些人奢谈友谊是疯狂而愚蠢的。美英之间仅存的那点亲密情感日渐消损。难道我们有理由希望，当二者之间的关系荡然无存的时候，它们的感情却与日俱增？或者，当我们就十倍于过去的更重大的事务争论时，意见反而会更加一致吗？

你们这些大谈和睦、和解的人，能使时间倒流吗？你们能使

① 马萨涅罗，又名托马斯·阿奈落，是意大利那不勒斯的一个渔民。当时，那不勒斯被西班牙占领，马萨涅罗在公共市场鼓动群众发动起义，反抗西班牙人的压迫。群众揭竿而起，马萨涅罗在一天之内就成了国王。——作者原注

娼妓恢复纯真吗？同样，你们也无法使英美和解。英美之间的最后一根纽带已经断裂，英国人正在大放厥词，发表敌对言论。这是上天也不能原谅的伤害；否则，上天就不成其为上天了。如果恋人能够宽恕强暴他情侣的暴徒，那么，美洲大陆就能原谅英国凶手。万能的上帝赋予我们不可遏制的情感，去追求美好与明智。这种情感就是我们心中上帝形象的守护者。它使我们区别于其他普通的动物。如果我们冷酷无情，社会契约就会终结，正义就会彻底灭绝或者只是昙花一现。如果我们所受到的伤害并没有促使我们去追求正义，那么，强盗和杀人凶手将多半会逃脱法网。

啊！你们这些热爱人类的人！你们这些不但敢反对暴政，而且敢反对暴君的人，请站到前面来！旧世界的每一个角落都充斥着压迫。在地球上，自由被到处逐猎。亚洲和非洲早就将她驱逐出境。欧洲把她视为异端。英国则对她发出了驱逐令。啊！接纳这个流亡者吧，及时为人类准备一个避难所吧！

第四章　对当前北美能力的看法及其他杂想

应该首先制定政府的各项规程或宪章，然后再授权一些人遵照执行。

无论在英国，还是在北美，我从未遇到过一个不认为这两个国家迟早必然分离的人。但是，在确定所谓的北美独立的成熟时机或适当时机的时候，我们却显得毫无判断力。

既然所有人都一致赞同这个方案，只是对时间的考虑有所不同，那么，为了避免错误，让我们对形势作个总体梳理，并尽可能确定合适的时点。其实，我们无需花费太多的精力，上述工作就嘎然而止，因为时间径自呈现在我们面前。社会共识和所有事件汇成的辉煌趋势都使之不言自明。

我们的力量不在于数量，而在于团结。当然，我们现在的人数足够击退全世界的兵力。北美大陆此刻拥有普天之下最庞大的装备精良、纪律严明的军队；而且，其力量刚好达到一个恰到好处的节点——此时，任何一个殖民地都无法单独自立；但是，它们联合起来作为一个整体却无往不利，其力量无论多一分，还是减一点，都可能造成致命的后果。我们的陆军已足够强大，说到海军，大家不可能没有意识到，只要英国人还掌控着北美大陆，就绝不会让我们发展海上力量。因此，在海军建设方面，即便是百年之后，也未必比当下更有成效。事实是，发展海军的客观条件会越来越差，因为我们的木材资源随着不断开采而日渐减少，最后剩下的那点不是藏于荒远之地，就是难以开采利用。

假如北美大陆人口众多，那她现在所遭受的苦难就是无法容忍的。我们的海港越多，需要防卫的城市就越多，而不得不放弃的城市也就越多。我们现在的人口恰好满足需要，没有人无所事事。减少贸易能够腾出人力补充兵员，而军需又催生了一门新的生意。我们没有债务，如果我们因独立而欠债，那将是我们德行的光荣纪念。只要我们能把一个固定的政府形式、一个独立且独特的政体留给子孙，付出任何代价都是物超所值。但是，如果花费数百万英镑只是为了撤销几项法案和推翻现任内阁，那就得不偿失了。而且，这是在用最残忍的方式对待我们的后代，因为我们留给后代一项未完成的艰巨工作，并使他们背上从中得不到任何好处的沉重的债务。这种想法对于有尊严的人来说，是不值一提的，但却是心胸狭窄的人和无聊政客的标签。

倘若我们的功业得以完成，债务是不足为虑的。任何一个国家都不应该没有债务。国债就是国家的证券，只要没有利息，就没什么大不了的。英国负债 1.4 亿多镑，应付利息 400 多万镑；但与此同时，它拥有一支强大的海军。北美没有债务，也没有海军。其实，我们只需花费英国国债的 1/20，就能拥有一支同样强大的海军。现在，英国海军的装备总价还不到 350 万英镑。

本书第一版和第二版未开列下面的相关数据，现将之整理出来，以证明上述对海军军备的估算是公允的（参见恩缇克[①]：《海军史》导言，第 56 页）。

根据海军部长波切特先生的计算，每一个级别军舰的造价以及装备桅杆、帆桁、船帆、索具的费用，还有按比例储备的水手和工匠航行 8 个月所需物资总计为：

单艘舰艇配备火炮数量（门）	军舰造价（镑）
100	35，553
90	29，886
80	23，638
70	17，785
60	14，197
50	10，606
40	7，558
30	5，846
20	3，710

---

① 约翰·恩缇克（约 1703—1773），英国作家。

我们据此可以很容易地推算出整个英国海军的装备造价，即海军成本。英国海军在 1757 年极盛时期拥有如下舰船与火炮：

舰艇数量	单艘舰艇配备火炮数量（门）	单艘造价（镑）	合计造价（镑）
6	100	35,533	213,318
12	90	29,886	358,632
12	80	23,638	283,656
43	70	17,785	746,755
35	60	14,197	496,895
40	50	10,606	424,240
45	40	7,558	344,110
58	20	3,710	215,180
单桅帆船、炸弹、炮艇共计 85 艘		2,000	170,000
合计			3,266,786
添置火炮的款项			233,214
总计			3,500,000

世界上没有哪个国家拥有北美这样优越的地理位置，也没有哪个国家像我们这样有能力建立一支舰队。柏油、木材、铁和绳索都是我们的特产，因此我们用不着从外国采购原材料。尽管荷兰人把自己的舰船租借给西班牙和葡萄牙，从中获取丰厚的利润，但是，他们却不得不从国外进口大部分造船原料。既然北美独具造船所需的充足的自然资源，我们就应该把建立舰队视为一笔生意。这是我们最好的投资，因为海军一旦建成，便会物超所

值。国家政策的优点就在于能将商业和国防统一起来。让我们建造一支舰队吧。如果不想要了，大可出售，换取真金白银取代我们的纸币来流通。

关于舰队的人员配备，人们大都陷入了一个很大的误区。其实，完全没有必要1/4的人都是水手。那艘可怕的海盗船"死神船长号"在上次战争中与所有遭遇船只都进行了激战。尽管其全员有200多人，但水手还不到20人。几个能干且善于沟通的水手很快就能指导足够多的、积极的新手进行船上的普通工作。现在，我们的木材供应充足，而渔场遭到封锁，水手和船匠陷于失业，这正是开启我们海洋事业的良机。40年前，我们曾经在新英格兰地区①建造了几艘装有七八十门火炮的战舰，为什么现在不去做同样的事情呢？造船是北美最值得骄傲的事业。总有一天，北美将在这个领域傲视全球。东方的伟大帝国大多位居内陆，因此不可能与北美较量。非洲尚是蛮荒之地。欧洲列强既没有我们这样漫长的海岸线，也没有丰富的物产资源。幅员辽阔的俄国几乎没有出海口，所以，它那无尽的森林、柏油、铁和绳索只不过是用来交易的商品罢了。通常情况下，鱼与熊掌不可兼得，大自然在一方面慷慨，必然在另一方面吝啬。偏偏北美得天独厚，受

---

① 新英格兰地区位于美国大陆东北角，包括缅因、新罕布什尔、佛蒙特、马萨诸塞、罗德岛、康涅狄格六地，是英国在北美最早进行殖民的地区。18世纪，新英格兰地区也是最早表达脱离英国独立愿望的英属北美殖民地之一。

到上天的青睐，占尽地利之便。

出于安全考虑，我们也应该有一支舰队。我们不再是60年前的那个不值一提的群体了。彼时，我们或许曾经放心大胆地把财物放在里巷之中，甚或田间陇上，门窗不锁也能酣然入梦。但是现在不一样了，我们的自卫手段应该随着财产的增加而提高。12个月以前，一个蹩脚的海盗就能沿着特拉华河①逆流而上，向费城的居民任意勒索巨款。同样的事情也可能在其他地方发生。更有甚者，一个胆大妄为之徒驾着一艘配备了14或16门火炮的双桅船就能洗劫整个北美大陆，抢走价值50万英镑的财物。这些情况唤起了我们的警觉，并指出了海防的必要性。

有些人可能会说，与英国和解之后，它会来保护我们的。难道我们竟愚蠢到认为英国会在我们的海港中驻军保护我们？显而易见，那种一直试图征服我们的力量是最不适合来保护我们的。征服将在友谊的幌子下实现；而我们在长期的英勇抵抗后，终将受到蒙骗沦为奴隶。况且，如果不让英国军舰进入我们的港口，它又怎么来保护我们呢？远在三四千英里之外的海军几乎毫无用处；面对突发的紧急事件，更是束手无策。因此，如果我们今后必须自卫，为什么不自力更生呢？为什么要依靠他人呢？

----

① 特拉华河是美国东北部的一条重要河流，发源于纽约州的卡茨基尔山，流入特拉华湾，特伦顿以下可以通航。沿岸主要城市有费城、特伦顿、伊斯顿等。

从名单上看，英国军舰数量众多，装备精良；但无论何时，其中只有不到 1/10 的船只可供使用。很多船已经不存在了，但是只要尚存一块船板，它们的名字就会虚张声势地出现在名单上。在尚可使用的船只中，只有不到 1/5 能够停泊在任何一个港口待命。东印度群岛、西印度群岛、地中海、非洲以及大英帝国版图内的其他角落，都对英国海军需求甚大。由于偏见和粗心大意，我们存在一种误解，觉得好像要同时与整个英国海军对抗似的，因此便认定，我们必须拥有一支同样强大的海军。这种不可能马上实行的办法曾被一小撮伪装起来的托利党人①利用，来阻挠我们着手建立海军。其实，这种看法荒谬绝伦，因为我们只要拥有相当于英国 1/20 的海军力量，便会成为英国的劲敌。因为我们既没有，也不妄图侵占任何他国领土，我们的所有海军都可以驻扎在自己的海岸线上。长远来看，我们较敌方占据了双倍的优势：他们不得不跋涉三四千英里，长途奔袭我们；还要经由同样的距离返航修整、补给。尽管英国舰队可以截断我们与欧洲的贸易，我们也可以阻挠它同毗邻北美大陆的西印度群岛之间的贸易。这个弹丸之地完全在我们的控制之下。

---

　　① 在美国历史上，北美独立前后主张效忠英王的亲英分子自称"亲英派"，支持独立的人称他们为"托利党"。与之对立的独立派被称为辉格党。此外，英国历史上也有一个政党叫托利党，诞生于 17 世纪，是英国政界的保守势力，后演变为英国保守党。

如果我们觉得没有必要在和平时期维持一支常备海军，则可采取某种变通办法保持兵力。比如，奖励商人建造并使用配备有20、30、40，或50门数量不等的火炮的船只（奖金数额与载炮所导致的船舱容积损失成正比）。五六十艘这样的船只，再加上几艘持续巡逻的警戒舰，就可以保持一支足够强大的海军力量。这样，我们也就不会遇到那个让英国人大伤脑筋的难题：和平时期，眼睁睁地看着舰队在船坞里腐烂。将商业资源与国防事业结合起来是非常有效的策略。因为当我们的实力与财富相辅相成的时候，就不必惧怕任何外敌了。

　　几乎任何一种国防物资在北美都储藏丰富。苎麻差不多随处可见，故而我们不缺索具。我们的铁优于其他各国。我们的轻武器不输于别国的产品。大炮更是可以随意制造。硝石和火药每天都在生产。我们的知识时时刻刻都在增加。意志坚定是我们与生俱来的品质，胆识、勇气从来没有离我们而去。我们还缺什么？我们为什么还在犹豫？除了毁灭之外，我们不能指望从英国得到任何东西。如果英国对北美的统治再次得到确认，这个大陆就不值得我们生活下去了。那时，将会猜忌四起，暴乱不断。谁能平息这一切？谁会冒着生命危险让自己的同胞屈从外国的统治？宾夕法尼亚和康涅狄格就几处未定疆界发生的争执，不但说明凌驾于北美之上的英国政府确实无足轻重，而且充分证明只有北美自己的政府才能管理北美的事务。

还有一个理由可以证明现在是独立的最佳时机。那就是：北美的人口越少，未被占领的土地就越多。那些处女地如果不被英王肆意赏赐给他那些卑劣的仆从，就会在今后得到开发利用，其收入不但可以偿还当前的债务，而且可以为政府提供稳定的经费来源。普天之下没有哪个国家具备这样得天独厚的条件。

　　所谓的北美殖民地的幼稚状态并不是反对独立的理由，而是支持独立的论据。我们的人口足够了，如果再多的话，就可能产生矛盾纷争。值得注意的是，一个国家人口越多，军队人数就越少。古代各国的兵力远远超过现代国家。其中的道理显而易见：人口增长带来贸易繁荣，人们专注于商业就无暇他顾了。商业削弱了人们的爱国精神和尚武精神。大量史实告诉我们，最勇敢无畏的功业总是一个国家在其未成年时完成的。随着商业贸易的发展，英国已经丧失了进取精神。伦敦尽管人口众多，但却怯懦地忍受着接连不断的侮辱。人们可能的损失越大，就越不愿去冒险。一般来说，有钱人都是胆小鬼，一副卑躬屈膝的小人嘴脸，战战兢兢、口是心非地屈从于宫廷权威。

　　青年时代是良好习惯的播种季节，对个人而言如此，对国家亦然。50年之后在北美大陆建立单一的政府，这个想法即便不是不可能的，也会很困难。随着时间的推移，贸易和人口增加导致的大量利益纷争将催生混乱，殖民地之间会争斗不止。各个殖民地均已自立，于是便忽视了互相帮助。当自负而愚蠢的人为点滴成绩得意洋洋的时候，智者却在痛惜之前未能结成联盟。眼下正是建立联盟的最佳时机。总角之交的亲密和风雨同舟的友谊是最持久和牢不可破的。北美目前的联盟具有如下特点：我们年轻，并曾经历苦难；团结使我们共度难关，并且创建了一个令子孙后代引以为荣的、值得纪念的国度。

当前也是一个特殊的时期——一个国家只有一次机会组织自己的政府。大部分国家错过了这个机会，只能被迫接受征服者强加给他们的法律，而不能给自己制定法律。这些国家都是先有国王，然后才组成某种形式的政府。其实，应该首先制定政府的各项规程或宪章，然后再授权一些人遵照执行。他国的教训让我们明白，应该抓住眼前的机会，按照正确的顺序组建政府。

威廉一世征服英伦的时候，用刀剑强迫英国人接受了他的法律。北美的政权在被合法且权威地掌握之前，存在着被某个走运的恶棍篡夺的危险。他会用威廉一世的方式对待我们。届时，我们的自由在何处？我们的财产又在哪里？

说到宗教，我认为，保护所有开诚布公宣布自己宗教信仰的人是一切政府不可推卸的责任。除此之外，我不知道政府在此方面还有什么别的职责。如果抛弃各行各业的吝啬鬼都执著固守的狭隘精神和原则上的自私，人们就会立刻摆脱恐惧。猜疑与卑鄙的灵魂相伴共生，也是一切美好社会的毒药。就我个人而言，我真诚而彻底地坚信，世间存在多种宗教信仰乃是上帝的意志。这也为展示基督教的仁爱宽厚提供了一个更广阔的舞台。假如我们大家只有一种思维方式，那就有必要考察何以出现不同的宗教倾向了。根据这个宽容的原则，我觉得，不同的教派就是一个家庭中的几个孩子，它们只不过教名不同罢了。

在前文中，我曾发表对《大陆宪章》性质的几点看法（我只打算抛砖引玉，而不是展示方案）。此处，我将再次提起这个话题。我认为，宪章应该是一种所有人都参与其中的神圣义务盟约，用以保障内部各部分在宗教、个人自由和财产方面的权利。牢固的契约和准确的账目可以保证友谊地久天长。我曾在前文中提及建立广泛而平等的代议制的必要性。再也没有比这更值得注意的政治问题了。选民少或代表少，都是危险的。如果代表不但人数少，而且不平等，则危险更甚。假设，当主张联合的人将请愿书提交到宾夕法尼亚州议会的时候，只有 28 名议员到会。巴克斯郡的所有 8 名议员全部投反对票，切斯特郡的 7 名议员也投反对票，于是，整个州就被区区两个郡操控了[①]。这种危险会经常出现。而议会在上一次开会时，非法延长会期，试图获得凌驾于代表之上的不当权力，这种僭越之举应当引起全体人民的警觉，看看他们自己是如何把权力交付出去的。给代表议员们的一套指示说明完全是东拼西凑起来的。无论从常识的角度，还是从专业

---

① 现在，美国宾夕法尼亚州共辖 66 郡，其中包括巴克斯郡和切斯特郡。据此推测，即便在 18 世纪中后期，这两个郡也肯定只能代表整个宾州的极少数。

的角度，这套东西连小学生都会觉得丢脸，但却在议会之外为极少数人同意后，被带进议会，以全州的名义获得通过。然而，如果全州人民获悉，议会在制定某些必要的公共措施时居心不良，肯定会毫不犹豫地认定议员们辜负了信任。

迫切的需要令我们不得不采取很多权宜之计，但如果不做修正继续使用，这些措施就会变为压迫。权变之举不见得是正当的。当北美面临危险，需要磋商解决的时候，最便捷或最合适的办法就是让几个州的议会指派人来共商大计。这些人所表现出的智慧曾使北美大陆免于毁灭。但是，我们不可能永远没有国会。每一个期待良好秩序的人都必须承认，应该认真考量遴选国会议员的方法。我要问研究人类的人们一个问题：让同一群人掌握代议权及选举权，他们的权力是否过大？长远来看，我们应该记住，德行并不遗传。我们常常从敌方获得精妙的箴言，并不时对他们的错误感到吃惊，进而开始理性地思考问题。康沃尔先生①（英国的财政大臣）因为纽约州议会只有 26 名议员，而对其请愿不屑一顾。他认为，区区这点人数，根本不能代表全体人民。我们要感谢他在无意中口吐真言②。

---

① 查尔斯·康沃尔（1735—1789），英国政治家。1774—1780 年在诺斯内阁中任财政大臣。

② 如想全面了解广泛而平等的代议制对一个州的重要性，请参阅伯格所著《政治研究》。——作者原注

总而言之，虽然有些人觉得独立的主张怪异陌生，虽然有些人不愿意接受这种看法，这都无所谓。诸多显而易见、不容置疑的理由说明，只有公开地断然宣布独立，才能迅速解决我们面临的种种问题。现列举几条理由如下：

第一，按照国际惯例，两国交战时，应由置身事外、无利益关联的第三方出面斡旋，提出合约草案。所以，只要北美仍自称大不列颠的臣属，任何国家，无论它是多么支持我们，都无法出面调解。而就目前情况来看，英美争端可能会永远持续下去。

第二，那种认为法国或西班牙会给我们提供任何形式帮助的看法是不切实际的。如果我们只是想利用这种帮助来修补裂痕，强化英美关系，将会给法、西两国带来严重的后果。

第三，只要我们自认为是英国的臣民，在外国人眼中，我们就是叛乱者。历史经验证明，以子民的身份揭竿而起反抗主上的行为，多多少少会给自己招来危险。我们现在就可以摆脱这种尴尬的身份。但是，如果想把抵抗与屈从结合起来，那就需要精深的奇思妙想了，绝非普通人所能理解。

第四，我们或可发表一份宣言，痛陈我们遭受的痛苦，列举我们为修复英美关系而采取的种种和平的、徒劳无益的办法；同时声明，鉴于我们不可能在英王的统治下过上幸福或安全的生活，我们不得不切断与英国的所有联系；另外，还要向各国表达寻求和平并开展贸易的愿望，然后，将之分送至各国政府。对于北美大陆而言，这样一份备忘录比运送一船请愿书到英国还有用。

顶着英国臣民的名号，我们既不会被世界各国接受，也不会有人倾听我们的呼声。国际惯例对我们不利，并将永远如此，直到我们通过独立使自己与其他各国平起平坐。

这些行动乍看上去似乎是异想天开，而且困难重重，但是，就像我们已经历的其他步骤那样，它们很快就会变得熟悉而可心了。在宣布独立之前，北美大陆就像这样一个人：他总是将某件烦心事一天天拖下去，但心里其实知道这事非做不可。他不愿动手，希望此事不了了之，但同时又念念不忘此事的必要性。

附录一　附记

自从这本小册子的初版问世以来，或者说，就在它面世的那天，英王的讲话也在城中①出现了。即便在先知的指引下，我们也找不到比这更合适的节点，或更有必要的时刻来出版此书。一方的嗜血残暴恰好证明另一方有必要采取应对措施。人们从英国的报复中认清了一切。英王的讲话非但没有吓倒我们，反而为果断的独立主张开辟了道路。

不论动机如何，无论是彬彬有礼甚或是沉默应对，人们只要对卑鄙邪恶的行为稍加辞色，就会产生严重的后果。如果大家认同这一看法的话，自然会发现，英王的讲话非常邪恶，无论是现在还是将来，都应受到国会和民众的一致咒骂。可是，由于这个

---

① 指费城。

国家的内部平静很大程度上依赖于被称为"民风"的那种淳朴，所以我们往往对某些事不屑一顾，用沉默表达轻蔑，而不是采用表示反感的新方法。而后者或许能为我们和平与安全的守护者带来点滴革新。很有可能，正是这种谨慎的微妙态度，使英王的讲话在此之前并未受到公众的谴责。如果尚可称为演讲的话，那篇东西也只不过是对真相、公共利益和人类生活的肆意攻击。它用一种头头是道、夸大其词的方式把人类献祭给暴君的骄横。当然，这种对人类的大屠杀正是君主的特权之一，也是君主掌权的必然后果。因为造化不了解君主，君主们也没有参透造化。虽然君主是我们自己的创造，可他们非但不了解我们，反而成了他们的创造者的神明。不过，英王的讲话有一个优点，那就是并没有处心积虑地欺骗我们。即便我们愿意上当，也不会被骗，因为其字里行间赤裸裸地充斥着残忍和专横，令我们绝对不会产生误解和迷惑。每一个阅读瞬间，每一行文字都让我们确信，英国国王比赤身裸体在树林中狩猎的未开化的印第安人更野蛮。

　　据说，约翰·达林默普爵士[①]就是那篇荒谬地题名为《英国人民致北美居民书》的怨天怨地的诡辩之词的作者。他可能想当然地觉得，北美人民会被他对国王的吹捧和描画吓倒，竟然清楚地勾勒出当今英王的真实性格（尽管对他来说，这是非常不明

---

　　① 约翰·达林默普（1726—1810），英国政治家、作家。

智的)。他这么写道:"但是,如果你想赞美一个令人满意的政府(指废除了《印花税法案》的罗金汉姆侯爵①内阁),但却没有称颂国王,这是非常不公平的。因为**只有国王点头,内阁成员才能做事**。"这是确凿的保守主义观点!赤裸裸的个人崇拜!能够平心静气接受这种主张的人不但丧失了理性,而且背弃了人伦秩序,他们甚至放弃了人类的尊严,将自己置于动物之下,像条毛毛虫似的在世间可鄙地爬行。

不过,无论英王说了什么,或做了什么,现在都无所谓了。他已经居心叵测地摧毁了一切人类道德和义务,践踏了人类的天性与良心,并因其一贯固有的傲慢与残忍招致公愤。眼下,北美的当务之急就是给自己寻找出路。北美殖民地已经组成了一个年轻的大家庭。我们的责任是照顾这个家庭,而不是慷慨地拿出财产去支持一个辱没了人类和基督徒之名的政权。无论皈依何门何派,我们都有责任守护国家的道德精神。此外,我们更是公共自由的守护者。如果有人力图保护自己的祖国不受欧洲腐败的侵染,那他内心深处一定渴望独立。除了将道德内容留给私人反省之外,我将主要对如下问题做进一步阐释:

首先,脱离英国而独立,符合北美大陆的利益。

---

① 查尔斯·沃森·温特沃斯(1730—1782),第二代罗金汉姆侯爵,英国辉格党政治家,曾两度出任英国首相。他在 1765 年继格伦威尔之后出任首相,最终说服国王,推动议会在 1766 年 3 月废除了《印花税法案》。

其次，和解或独立，究竟哪种方案更容易，更具可行性呢？我将再做些补充说明。

为了论证第一个问题，我可以转述一下我所理解的北美大陆最才华出众、最经验丰富的人的意见。尽管他们的主张尚未公诸于众，但其实是显而易见的。因为任何一个依附于外的国家，贸易必然受到限制，立法权也会受到束缚，将永远无法实现强国之梦。相较于其他各国，北美已完成的发展是无可比拟的，但这片大陆还不知道什么是富裕。如果我们自己掌握了立法权（这是应该的），那么，北美现在的发展状况与可能实现的前景相比，也就是刚刚起步的雏形。英国正在傲慢地觊觎着即使得到也对自己全无益处的东西。而北美大陆正对一个如被忽略就会导致其灰飞烟灭的问题犹疑不定。英国的利益在于与北美进行贸易，而不是征服北美。如果英、美像法国和西班牙那样各自独立的话，两国的贸易关系大体会保持下去。因为具体到很多商品，英、美都是彼此最好的市场。北美大陆脱离英国或任何其他国家独立，是当下主要的，也是唯一值得讨论的问题。这一点就像其他必然被发现的真理一样，将会日渐清晰、有力地呈现在世人面前。

因为它迟早会产生这样的结果。

因为拖延的时间越长，完成起来就越困难。

在公共集会和私人聚会上，我常常以默默地聆听信口开河者谬妄无稽的言论为乐。在我听到的种种谬论中，下面这个最常见，即，如果在四五十年之后，而不是现在与英国决裂，北美将更有可能摆脱从属地位。对此，我的答复是，我们现在的军事实力得自上次战争①，四五十年后，一切都会消亡殆尽。到那时，北美大陆将不复有一名将军，甚至都没有一位军官。而我们，或者是我们的子孙，对军事知识将会像古老的印第安人一样无知。想想吧，单凭这一点就无可争辩地证明，现在就是独立的最佳时机。于是，论证就变成了这样：在上次战争结束时，我们有了经验，但人手不足；四五十年之后，我们将人员充足，但却缺乏经验。因此，最佳时点就是上次战争与四五十年后之间的某个特定一点。此时，我们既有经验，又有足够的人手。这便是此时此刻。

请读者们原谅我这些并非由最初议题引发的题外话，我们现在回到本题：

如果我们与英国修复关系，让它继续享有北美的统治权和主权（随着形势的发展，北美正在彻底放弃这种主张），就使自己失去了还债或再行借款的途径。由于加拿大疆域的无理扩张②，北

---

① 在1756—1763年进行的七年战争期间，英属北美殖民地参加了英国在今俄亥俄一带与法国人、印第安人进行的战争。关于七年战争的情况，请参见第68页注①。

② 英国议会在1774年颁布了旨在加强对魁北克统治的《魁北克法案》，将英属北美13个殖民地以西的俄亥俄河流域和伊利诺伊地区划入魁北克的管辖范围，限制了北美殖民地的向西扩张，损害了北美殖民地的利益，激化了反英情绪。

美殖民地已经蒙受了损失。如果以每百英亩价值 5 英镑计算，折合宾夕法尼亚币①值已达 2500 万镑以上；免役税以每英亩 1 便士计算，每年有 200 万镑之多。

出售这些土地即可偿还债务，消除负担；而所收免役税能减轻并迟早完全承担年度政府开支。还债时限不拘长短，只要售卖土地的收入被用于还债即可。目前，这些事务可以委托大陆会议处理。

现在，我们来讨论第二个议题，即，和解或独立，究竟哪种方案更容易，更具可行性呢？

遵循自然规律行事的人很难被驳倒。以此为基础，我对上述问题的回答是：**独立是一个唯一的、简单的路线**，只涉及我们自己；而和解则是一个极其错综复杂的问题，有一个背信弃义、反复无常的宫廷参与其中。我想，答案不言自明。

任何一个有思考能力的人都会对北美的现状感到深深的忧虑。没有法律，没有政府，除了基于恩惠也得之于恩惠的权力外，没有任何其他形式的权力。仅靠一种史无前例的凝聚力将我们大家团结在一起。但是，这种精神维系并不牢固，每一个隐秘的敌人都在试图瓦解它。我们目前的情况是：有立法而无法律；有智慧而无计划；有政体而无名称；最令人震惊的是，明明拥有

---

① 当时，英属北美殖民地已发行了自己的纸币。1764 年，英国议会通过的《货币法案》要求殖民地停止发行纸币，并令其限期停用当前流通的货币。

理想的独立性却非要依附于他人。这可真是前无古人！谁又能预料结果会怎样呢？在当前无规无矩的状态下，任何人的财产都没有保障。百姓都持从众心理，随波逐流，既然没有既定目标，他们便追求虚幻的或众口一词的东西。无所谓犯罪，也无所谓叛国，每个人都觉得可以为所欲为。如果那些亲英分子知道，根据国法，公然聚众会丢掉性命的话，他们肯定不敢这么干。我们应该在被俘英军士兵和持械北美居民之间划清界限，前者是俘虏，后者是叛徒；一个应被囚禁，另一个应被砍头。

尽管我们不乏智慧，但某些行动却明显不力。这导致分歧增大。"大陆的腰带"系得太松了。如果不及时采取措施，一切都将大势已去。到时，我们将陷入既不能和解，又不能独立的两难境地。英王和他那些不足挂齿的仆从正故伎重施分裂北美大陆。我们的出版商中也不乏忙于散布似是而非谎言的人。几个月前，出现在纽约两份报纸上以及另外两家报纸上的那封阴险狡诈、虚情假意的信札证明有些人既无判断力，又不诚实。

躲在洞穴和角落中大谈和解很容易。不过，"和解派"们是否仔细掂量过，这项事业有多么困难？如果北美大陆因此而分裂将会多么危险？他们是否意识到，除了自己，其他各色人等的情况也都应被考虑在内？他们是否与已然一无所有的受难者感同身受？他们是否设身处地地站在那些为保卫国家而牺牲一切的战士的立场上？如果和解派主张的不当的克制只是出于自身的考量，而完全不顾他人，形势的发展将让他们明白，"他们是未经同意，擅作主张"。

有人说，让我们回到 1763 年吧①。对此，我的回答是：现在，英国既不能满足这个要求，也不会提出这种建议。如果英国能够，甚至满足了这个要求，我就要顺理成章地追问："这样一个贪污腐败、两面三刀的宫廷如何能够履行义务？"下届议会，不，甚至就是本届议会，将绞尽脑汁地想办法取消它。他们或以用暴力手段获得为借口，或声称当初的决定不明智而断然撕毁约定，拒不履行义务。面对这种情况，我们又能怎样？根本无法求诸法律，大炮就是国王的律师。决定诉讼输赢的是战争，而不是公平正义。要想回到 1763 年，仅仅让法律回到从前是不够的，我们的生活环境也要恢复原貌：被火焚、摧毁的市镇应得到修复、重建；我们的个人损失应得到补偿；我们为保卫家园而欠下的公债应得到免除，否则，我们的生活将比那个令人羡慕的时代糟糕百万倍。如果这样的要求在一年前得到满足的话，英国原本可以赢得北美大陆的全心拥戴，但现在为时已晚，我们已经"渡过卢

---

① 1756—1763 年，欧洲主要国家以英国与法国为首，形成两大战争集团，在欧洲、北美、印度等广大地区展开争夺殖民地和贸易控制权的战争，史称七年战争。最终，英国取得了胜利。1763 年，双方签订《巴黎条约》，战争结束。条约规定，在北美地区，法国将整个加拿大、密西西比河以东的全部法国领土割给英国，只有新奥尔良除外。由此，英国控制了整个北美地区。

比孔河"①了。

除此之外，为了取消一项财政法令而动用武力，就像用武力来推行法令那样，似乎既不被神法所允许，也为人情所反感。生命极其珍贵，不应被浪费在微不足道的小事上，所以，无论从哪方面来说，都不能为达目的不择手段。用暴力威胁并伤及我们，用武力破坏我们的财产，用刀剑炮火入侵我们的祖国，这一切都坚定了我们揭竿而起、武力反抗的信念。一旦武装自卫成为必要，我们就不应再对英国俯首贴耳。北美独立应被视为打响了反英的第一枪；而这一枪也宣告了北美的独立。这条线索前后贯穿，始终一致，既不是任意行事，也不受野心驱使，而是由一系列并非由殖民地挑起的事件连结而成。

我们将用下面这些适时而善意的提醒结束本文。我们应当认识到，北美大陆可以采取三种方式实现独立，我们的选择迟早将决定北美的命运。这三种方式分别是：通过人民在议会中的合法呼声；使用武装力量；发动群众暴动。我们的士兵并不总是公民，民众也并不总是理智的。正像我早已言明的那样，德行不遗

---

① 在西方世界，"渡过卢比孔河"是一句很常用的成语，意为"破釜沉舟，义无反顾"。此语典出凯撒。根据当时罗马共和国的法律，任何将领都不得率军越过作为意大利本土与高卢分界线的卢比孔河，否则以叛变论处。这确保罗马共和国不会遭到来自内部的攻击。因此，公元前49年，时任高卢总督的凯撒率军渡过卢比孔河进入意大利的时候，就意味着挑起了针对元老院的内战，并将自己置于叛国者的地位。据说，凯撒在渡河前也曾犹豫过，但最终还是挥师渡河，进军罗马，战胜了庞培。

传，也不是一成不变的。如果采用第一种方式实现独立，我们就拥有各种机会并得到鼓励去建立世界上最宏伟、最廉洁的政体。我们有力量重建世界。自从诺亚时代①以来，还从未出现过现在的形势。一个新世界的诞生近在咫尺，一个人口约略相当于全欧洲总和的民族将从几个月发生的事件中获得自己的自由。这令人心生敬畏。相较于事关全世界的大计，一小撮懦弱之辈或利欲熏心之徒鼓噪的毫无价值的吹毛求疵是多么的微不足道，荒谬可笑啊！

　　如果我们忽视眼前这个有利的、诱人的时机，之后再采用其他方式取得独立，就只能自食恶果。也许，那些心胸狭隘、心存偏见的人更应对此负责。他们总是习惯性地反对独立，却从未进行调查研究，也没有认真思考过。赞同独立的若干理由应当了然于心，而不应被公开地告知。我们现在不应争论是否要独立，而应力求在坚固、稳定、正当的基础上实现独立，还应为尚未着手推进此事而感到忧虑。每一天，我们都更加确信独立的必要性。而托利党人（如果我们中间尚有这类人的话）应当是最热心的推

---

　　① 《圣经·创世纪》中有"诺亚方舟"的故事。上帝认为人类罪孽深重，要将所造的人和走兽并昆虫以及空中的飞鸟都从地上消灭，只有诺亚一人在上帝面前蒙恩。上帝选中了诺亚一家，作为新一代人类的种子保存下来。上帝告诉他们要用洪水实施大毁灭，要他们造一只方舟避难用。然后，洪水暴发，万物毁灭，只有方舟里的人和动物安然无恙。

动者。因为，当初委员会①的成立保护他们免于被群众的愤怒所伤，所以，一个了解民情且组织完善的政府将是继续保卫其安全的唯一可靠手段。因此，倘若他们的德行不够使其成为辉格党②人，那就应该深谋远虑，权衡利弊去追求独立。

简而言之，独立是唯一将我们连结并维系在一起的纽带。那时，我们将看清自己的目标，我们的耳朵将不再听信诡谲残忍的敌人的阴谋诡计。而且，我们也将采取合适的立场与英国打交道。因为我们有理由相信，英国宫廷与北美联邦磋商和平协议条款远比与它称之为"乱臣贼子"的人谈判和解条件保留了更多颜面。我们的拖延助长了英国征服北美的贪念，我们的退缩只会延长战争。我们曾经中断对英贸易进行反制，但徒劳无功。现在，我们不妨改弦更张，独立地处理此事，然后开放贸易。英国商人和通情达理的人仍会站在我们这边，因为保持贸易的和平远比中断贸易的战争更好。如果这个提议未被接受，我们可向其他国家提出。

我就是在上述基础上讨论、解决问题的。至今，尚没有人反驳这本小册子的前几版中的观点。这从反面证明，要么我的观点

① 应该指的是美国独立战争爆发前，北美各地出现的"自由之子"、"通讯委员会"等反英组织。

② 在美国历史上，"辉格党"指的是在独立战争前后主张暴力反抗英国统治的人，又称爱国者、大陆会议派。在英国历史上，也有一个名为"辉格党"的政党。英国辉格党诞生于 17 世纪末，19 世纪中叶演变为英国自由党。

不容置疑；要么支持我的人数量巨大，无法反对。因此，不要再怀疑观望了，让我们把热诚的友谊之手伸向邻居，团结一致，画出一条线，一条遗忘之线，埋葬并忘却之前的所有分歧异见。让辉格党、托利党之名从此烟消云散；让我们之间只有如下称呼存在：好公民、坦诚坚定的朋友、品德高尚的**人权**和**自由独立的北美联邦**的支持者。

附录二 致贵格会教徒书

教友派，又称贵格会①。本文即写给贵格会教徒，或是他们之中热衷于刊布最近公诸于众的那篇文章的人。此文名曰：《**就国王、政府**以及蔓延北美的骚乱，**贵格会教徒**以自己**古老的证言和原则告全体人民书**》。

笔者属于从未通过愚弄或指责任何派别来侮辱宗教的少数人之一。在宗教范畴，所有人都只对上帝负责，而不对任何人负责。因此，撰写此文时把你们视为宗教团体是不合适的，还是将你们看作一个政治团体吧。你们只是不经意涉足了自己所奉行的平静原则禁止参与的事务。

---

① 贵格会，又称公谊会或教友派，是基督教新教的一个派别，创立于17世纪的英国。该派反对任何形式的战争和暴力，主张人人生而平等，奉行和平主义和宗教自由。

既然你们未经授权，就矫称自己代表全体贵格会教徒，为了与你们平等对话，笔者不得不径自代表那些与你们大作观点相左的人。我还选择了特别的情境，以便你们在我身上发现自己不具备的品格，因为，无论你我，都没有政治代表权。

　　当人们误入歧途时，肯定会磕磕绊绊，甚至失足跌倒。从你们处理《告全体人民书》的方式来看，政治显然不是你们（作为一个宗教团体）应走之路。尽管你们自以为措辞得体，但是，该文就是一篇鱼目混珠的堆砌之作，在此基础上得出的结论，既不顺理成章，也不公平合理。

　　我们赞同《告全体人民书》前两页（全文不到 4 页）的观点，并且希望也能得到你们以礼相待，因为仁爱及对和平的向往并非贵格会所独有，而是所有教派信徒的自然的宗教渴望。在此基础上，当致力于建立我们自己的独立的政体的时候，我们便在希望、目的和目标方面超越了其他人。我们期待永久的和平。与英国的纷争令我们厌倦，只有彻底独立才能结束这一切。为了永久的、持续的和平，我们坚持不懈，背负着今天的罪恶和重担。我们正在，并将一步步继续推进独立，切断那种令我们血流成河的关系。这种关系哪怕仅存名义，也会是英美未来祸端的致命起因。

　　我们的战斗既不为复仇，也不为征服；既不出于自负，也不因于激情。我们没有指挥舰队和军队欺凌世界，也没有洗劫全球。我们在自己的葡萄架下受到攻击；在自己的家中，在自己的田垄上被人施暴。我们视敌人为车匪路霸、入室窃贼，既然无法用民法保护自己，那就只好用军法惩罚敌人。我们的武器将由你们之前使用的绞索改为刀剑。或许，我们同情、理解北美各地的被伤害者和被侮辱者，而你们中的一部分人心里缺少一分慈悲。请你们确认自己没有弄错《告全体人民书》的动机和基础。千万不要把冷酷的灵魂称为宗教，也不要让固执偏狭之人作为基督徒的代表。

啊，你们这些心怀成见的教徒只认同自己知道的原则！如果拿起武器就是犯罪，那么，首先挑起战争的人就更是罪大恶极。这两者的区别在于，一方是蓄意进攻，另一方则是忍无可忍的正当防卫。

因此，如果你们确实想真诚地感化世界，而不是把自己的宗教变成政治玩物，就应该向我们那些同样手拿**武器**的敌人宣讲你们的信条。只有这样，你们才能说服整个世界。拿出证据证明你们的真诚吧：到圣詹姆斯①刊发你们的大作，将之递交给驻波士顿的英军总司令以及正在劫掠我们沿海市镇的海军将军和船长们，还有那些在你们效忠的英王的权威下为非作歹、杀人如麻的

----

① 圣詹姆斯，英国地名，位于伦敦市中心的威斯敏斯特区，直到二战时期一直是英国最重要、最著名的贵族聚居区。

恶棍们。如果你们有巴克莱①那样真诚的灵魂，就应该历数英王的恶行，劝诫他改过，并警告他执迷不悟将会万劫不复。你们不应徇私偏袒，单单责备被伤害、被侮辱的人，而应该像虔诚的牧师那样，大声疾呼，不姑息一人。不要抱怨你们受到迫害，也不要觉得谴责来自我们，这一切都是你们咎由自取。我们直言不讳地宣布，之所以指责你们，不是因为你们是贵格会教徒，而是因为你们假装是，但却根本**不是贵格会教徒**。

唉！你们大作某些部分的特殊倾向以及你们的某些行动似乎将所有罪恶归结并理解为拿起武器这个行为，而且单指人民一方拿起武器。我们觉得，因为你们的行动方向缺乏一致性，所以，你们大概误把党派成见当作良知。我们也很难赞同你们那些装腔作势的顾虑。因为提出这些顾虑的人，一边宣称自己视金钱如粪土，一边对财富紧追不舍——步履坚定如时间，欲望强烈如死神。

在你们大作的第二页上引用了《旧约·箴言篇》的话："人

① "你既曾一帆风顺，也曾遭遇不幸；你清楚地知道被驱出国门的滋味；你既被人统治过，也曾头戴王冠君临天下。既然曾经压迫，你应该知道，无论对上帝来说，还是在凡人眼中，压迫者现在是多么可恨。在所有警告、昭示之后，如果你不但没有全心全意地皈依上帝，反而将上帝在你艰难之时的眷顾抛在脑后，声色犬马，骄奢淫逸，那将必然受到严厉的惩罚。那些将要或正在诱惑你的人会把你引向邪恶。不要落入他们的彀中。而最好、最常用的救治办法就是接受耶稣基督洒入你良心的光芒。这神圣之光既不能，也不会献媚于你，更不会任凭你在罪恶之中心安理得。"（《巴克莱致查理二世书》）——作者原注

所行的若蒙耶和华喜悦，耶和华也使他的仇敌与他和好。"你们摘录此话实在是不明智，因为它恰好证明，英王的所作所为（你们热切地希望支持他）并未"蒙耶和华喜悦"，否则，他的统治就应该是稳定安宁的。

现在，我们来讨论你们大作的后一部分。相对而言，之前的所有内容似乎都只是绪论而已：

"自从我们受到召唤，皈依耶稣基督的光辉，我们的良心呈现出的判断和原则始终是：建立和颠覆国王、政府是上帝独有的特权，出于上帝知晓的原因而发生。我们凡夫俗子不应插手此事，也不要僭越身份去谋划摧毁或推翻国王。我们应为国王、国家安全和所有人的利益祈祷：愿我们在所有的仁慈和诚实之中，在上帝欣喜地安排给我们的政府的统治下，过上和平宁静的生活。"如果这真是你们的原则，你们自己为什么不遵照执行呢？你们为什么不放下你们所谓的上帝的特权，让上帝自己处理呢？这些原则告诉你们，要耐心谦恭地等待所有公共事件的自然结果，并将之视作神意而接受。假如你们完全相信自己的观点，看看你们选择了一个怎样的发表时机啊！发表宣言本身就说明，要么你们口是心非，根本不相信自己的言论；要么你们德行不够而无法践行自己的观点。

贵格会的宗旨原则明显倾向于把人塑造成最安静、最温和的臣民——无论在什么样的政府统治之下。如果建立和颠覆国王、政府是上帝独有的特权，我们就无法侵夺祂的权利；而且，你们也就应该对围绕国王发生的或可能发生的各种事件表示赞同。奥利佛·克伦威尔①感谢你们。因为据此而言，查理一世就是死于上帝之手了。如果眼前这个查理一世的骄纵的模仿者②也同样死于非命的话，《告全体人民书》的作者和出版者只能自食其果，对此鼓掌欢呼了。国王们不是被神迹带离凡尘的；政体的变化也不是用世俗之外的什么手段取得的，而是得之于我们当下使用的手段。即便是救世主早已预言的驱逐犹太人的行动，也需武力才能实现。因此，既然你们拒绝支持一方，就不应该干预另一方，而应静待事态发展。万能的上帝创造了新世界，并尽可能遥远地将之与旧世界分置于东西两端。除非你们另有神意证明，这样的安排反映出上帝不赞成北美脱离腐败堕落的英国而独立；否则，你们如何才能根据自己的原则证明令人群情振奋的"因对所有这些文字、措施的憎恨而牢牢地团结在一起，这些措施和文字力图截断我们至今享有的与大不列颠王国的幸福联系，并阻止我们对英王及合法地居于其权威之下的那些人表达应有的、必要的

---

① 奥利佛·克伦威尔（1599—1658），英国资产阶级革命的领袖、政治家。在英国资产阶级革命中，他率军击败王军，并处死国王查理一世，宣布建立共和国。

② 指当时的英王乔治三世，1760—1820年在位。当时的北美人认为乔治三世是个邪恶残忍的暴君。1793年，乔治三世派遣使臣马嘎尔尼到中国，觐见了乾隆皇帝。

顺从"。这真是迎面一记耳光！在上一段中安静、驯服地将任命、更换、废黜国王和政府的大权交于上帝之手的人，现在想收回权利，参与这些重大事务。我们恰当引用的结论难道来自既定的原则？这其中的矛盾触目惊心，令人无法忽视；其荒谬匪夷所思，令人忍俊不禁。只有被一个绝望政党的心胸狭隘、满腹抱怨的颓败蒙蔽了理解力的人才能得出这样的结论。你们不是贵格会教徒的全体，而只是其中的一派，微不足道的一部分。

　　我对你们大作的分析到此为止（我并没有鼓动任何人憎恨你们的所作所为，只是让读者自己阅读并进行公正的判断），现仅做如下补充："扶立和推翻国王"无疑是指，让一个尚非国王的人成为国王，令一个已是国王的人摘下王冠。那么，这与北美当前的形势有什么关系？我们既不打算扶立国王，也不打算推翻国王；既不打算让一个不是国王的人登上王位，也不打算让一个国王交出权杖。我们的计划与此全无干系。因此，无论从哪个角度看，你们的大作都只是展示了你们自己低下的判断力。考虑到其他因素，奉劝你们最好将之藏于名山，而不要公诸于众。

　　首先，因为这会引起对宗教的贬抑和指责，并使宗教成为政治争论中的一个因素。而这对社会来说是极其危险的。

　　其次，因为这反映出，一部分人反对发表那份政治宣言，但却被卷入其中并被胁迫而成为支持者。

　　再次，因为这会破坏北美大陆的和谐与友谊。你们近来慷慨仁慈的捐献对这种和谐、友谊的建立大有裨益，而保持这种和谐、友谊对我们所有人都是极其重要的。

现在，我要毫无怨愤地与你们告别了。我真诚地希望，作为人，作为基督徒，你们能够全面而连续地享有所有民权与宗教权利，并进而帮助他人享有这些权利。但是，你们却不明智地将宗教与政治混为一谈。这可能会招致所有北美居民的否定与谴责。

Common Sense

Thomas Paine

Introduction

PERHAPS the sentiments contained in the following pages, are not yet sufficiently fashionable to procure them general favor; a long habit of not thinking a thing wrong, gives it a superficial appearance of being right, and raises at first a formidable outcry in defence of custom. But tumult soon subsides. Time makes more converts than reason.

As a long and violent abuse of power is generally the means of calling the right of it in question, (and in matters too which might never have been thought of, had not the sufferers been aggravated into the inquiry,) and as the king of England hath undertaken in his own right, to support the parliament in what he calls theirs, and as the good people of this country are grievously oppressed by the combination, they have an undoubted privilege to inquire into the pretensions of both, and equally to reject the usurpations of either.

In the following sheets, the author hath studiously avoided every thing which is personal among ourselves. Compliments as well as censure to individuals make no part thereof. The wise and the worthy need not the triumph of a pamphlet; and those whose sentiments are injudicious or unfriendly, will cease of themselves, unless too much pains is bestowed upon their conversion.

The cause of America is, in a great measure, the cause of all mankind. Many circumstances hath, and will arise, which are not local, but universal, and through which the principles of all lovers of mankind are affected, and in the event of which, their affections are interested. The laying a country desolate with fire and sword, declaring war against the natural rights of all mankind, and extirpating the defenders thereof from the face of the earth, is the concern of every man to whom nature hath given the power of feeling; of which class, regardless of party censure, is THE AUTHOR.

Philadelphia, February 14, 1776

Of the Origin and Design of Government in General, with Concise Remarks on the English Constitution

Some writers have so confounded society with government, as to leave little or no distinction between them; whereas they are not only different, but have different origins. Society is produced by our wants, and government by our wickedness; the former promotes our happiness positively by uniting our affections, the latter negatively by restraining our vices. The one encourages intercourse, the other creates distinctions. The first is a patron, the last a punisher.

Society in every state is a blessing, but government even in its best state is but a necessary evil; in its worst state an intolerable one; for when we suffer, or are exposed to the same miseries by a government, which we might expect in a country without government, our calamities is heightened by reflecting that we furnish the means by which we suffer. Government, like dress, is the badge of lost innocence; the palaces of kings are built on the ruins of the bowers of paradise. For were the impulses of conscience clear, uniform, and irresistibly obeyed, man would need no other lawgiver; but that not being the case, he finds it necessary to surrender up a part of his property to furnish means for the protection of the rest; and this he is induced to do by the same prudence which in every other case advises him out of two evils to choose the least. Wherefore, security being the true design and end of government, it unanswerably follows that whatever form thereof appears most likely to ensure it to us, with the least expense and greatest benefit, is preferable to all others.

In order to gain a clear and just idea of the design and end of government, let us suppose a small number of persons settled in some sequestered part of the earth, unconnected with the rest, they will then represent the first peopling of any country, or of the world. In this state of natural liberty, society will be their first thought. A thousand motives will excite them thereto, the strength of one man is so unequal to his wants, and his mind so unfitted for perpetual solitude, that he is soon obliged to seek assistance and relief of another, who in his turn requires the same. Four or five united would be able to raise a tolerable dwelling in the midst of a wilderness, but one man might labour out the common period of life without accomplishing any thing; when he had felled his timber he could not remove it, nor erect it after it was removed; hunger in the mean time would urge him from his work, and every different want call him a different way. Disease, nay even misfortune would be death, for though neither might be mortal, yet either would disable him from living, and reduce him to a state in which he might rather be said to perish than to die.

Thus necessity, like a gravitating power, would soon form our newly arrived emigrants into society, the reciprocal blessings of which, would supersede, and render the obligations of law and government unnecessary while they remained perfectly just to each other; but as nothing but heaven is impregnable to vice, it will unavoidably happen, that in proportion as they surmount the first difficulties of emigration, which bound them together in a common cause, they will begin to relax in their duty and attachment to each other; and this remissness will point out the necessity, of establishing some form of government to supply the defect of moral virtue.

Some convenient tree will afford them a State-House, under the branches of which, the whole colony may assemble to deliberate on public matters. It is more than probable that their first laws will have the title only of Regulations, and be enforced by no other penalty than public disesteem. In this first parliament every man, by natural right will have a seat.

But as the colony increases, the public concerns will increase likewise, and the distance at which the members may be separated, will render it too inconvenient for all of them to meet on every occasion as at first, when their number was small, their habitations near, and the public concerns few and trifling. This will point out the convenience of their consenting to leave the legislative part to be managed by a select number chosen from the whole body, who are supposed to have the same concerns at stake which those hath who appointed them, and who will act in the same manner as the whole body would act were they present. If the colony continue increasing, it will become necessary to augment the number of the representatives, and that the interest of every part of the colony may be attended to, it will be found best to divide the whole into convenient parts, each part sending its proper number; and that the elected might never form to themselves an interest separate from the electors, prudence will point out the propriety of having elections often; because as the elected might by that means return and mix again with the general body of the electors in a few months, their fidelity to the public will be secured by the prudent reflection of not making a rod for themselves. And as this frequent interchange will establish a common interest with every part of the community, they will mutually and naturally support each other, and on this (not on the unmeaning name of king) depends the strength of government, and the happiness of the governed.

Here then is the origin and rise of government; namely, a mode rendered necessary by the inability of moral virtue to govern the world; here too is the design and end of government, viz. freedom and security. And however our eyes may be dazzled with snow, or our ears deceived by sound; however prejudice may warp our wills, or interest darken our understanding, the simple voice of nature and of reason will say, it is right.

I draw my idea of the form of government from a principle in nature, which no art can overturn, viz. that the more simple any thing is, the less liable it is to be disordered; and the easier repaired when disordered; and with this maxim in view, I offer a few remarks on the so much boasted constitution of England. That it was noble for the dark and slavish times in which it was erected is granted.

When the world was overrun with tyranny the least remove therefrom was a glorious rescue. But that it is imperfect, subject to convulsions, and incapable of producing what it seems to promise, is easily demonstrated.

Absolute governments (though the disgrace of human nature) have this advantage with them, that they are simple; if the people suffer, they know the head from which their suffering springs, know likewise the remedy, and are not bewildered by a variety of causes and cures. But the constitution of England is so exceedingly complex, that the nation may suffer for years together without being able to discover in which part the fault lies; some will say in one and some in another, and every political physician will advise a different medicine.

I know it is difficult to get over local or long standing prejudices, yet if we will suffer ourselves to examine the component parts of the English constitution, we shall find them to be the base remains of two ancient tyrannies, compounded with some new republican materials.

First. The remains of monarchical tyranny in the person of the king.

Secondly. The remains of aristocratical tyranny in the persons of the peers.

Thirdly. The new republican materials in the persons of the commons, on whose virtue depends the freedom of England.

The two first, by being hereditary, are independent of the people; wherefore in a constitutional sense they contribute nothing towards the freedom of the state.

To say that the constitution of England is a union of three powers reciprocally checking each other, is farcical, either the words have no meaning, or they are flat contradictions.

To say that the commons is a check upon the king, presupposes two things:

First. That the king is not to be trusted without being looked after, or in other words, that a thirst for absolute power is the natural disease of monarchy.

Secondly. That the commons, by being appointed for that purpose, are either wiser or more worthy of confidence than the crown.

But as the same constitution which gives the commons a power to check the king by withholding the supplies, gives afterwards the king a power to check the commons, by empowering him to reject their other bills; it again supposes that the king is wiser than those whom it has already supposed to be wiser than him. A mere absurdity!

There is something exceedingly ridiculous in the composition of monarchy; it first excludes a man from the means of information, yet empowers him to act in cases where the highest judgment is required. The state of a king shuts him from the world, yet the business of a king requires him to know it thoroughly; wherefore the different parts, unnaturally opposing and destroying each other, prove the whole character to be absurd and useless.

Some writers have explained the English constitution thus: the king, say they, is one, the people another; the peers are a house in behalf of the king, the commons in behalf of the people; but this hath all the distinctions of a house divided against itself; and though the expressions be pleasantly arranged, yet when examined they appear idle and ambiguous; and it will always happen, that the nicest construction that words are capable of, when applied to the description of something which either cannot exist, or is too incomprehensible to be within the compass of description, will be words of sound only, and though they may amuse the ear, they cannot inform the mind, for this explanation includes a previous question, viz. How came the king by a power which the people are afraid to trust, and always obliged to check? Such a power could not be the gift of a wise people, neither can any power, which needs checking, be from God; yet the provision, which the constitution makes, supposes such a power to exist.

But the provision is unequal to the task; the means either cannot or will not accomplish the end, and the whole affair is a felo de se; for as the greater weight will always carry up the less, and as all the wheels of a machine are put in motion by one, it only remains to know which power in the constitution has the most weight, for that will govern;

and though the others, or a part of them, may clog, or, as the phrase is, check the rapidity of its motion, yet so long as they cannot stop it, their endeavours will be ineffectual; the first moving power will at last have its way, and what it wants in speed is supplied by time.

That the crown is this overbearing part in the English constitution, needs not be mentioned, and that it derives its whole consequence merely from being the giver of places and pensions is self-evident, wherefore, though we have been wise enough to shut and lock a door against absolute monarchy, we at the same time have been foolish enough to put the crown in possession of the key.

The prejudice of Englishmen, in favour of their own government by king, lords, and commons, arises as much or more from national pride than reason. Individuals are undoubtedly safer in England than in some other countries, but the will of the king is as much the law of the land in Britain as in France, with this difference, that instead of proceeding directly from his mouth, it is handed to the people under the more formidable shape of an act of parliament. For the fate of Charles the First, hath only made kings more subtle not more just.

Wherefore, laying aside all national pride and prejudice in favour of modes and forms, the plain truth is, that it is wholly owing to the constitution of the people, and not to the constitution of the government, that the crown is not as oppressive in England as in Turkey.

An inquiry into the constitutional errors in the English form of government is at this time highly necessary; for as we are never in a proper condition of doing justice to others, while we continue under the influence of some leading partiality, so neither are we capable of doing it to ourselves while we remain fettered by any obstinate prejudice. And as a man, who is attached to a prostitute, is unfitted to choose or judge of a wife, so any prepossession in favor of a rotten constitution of government will disable us from discerning a good one.

Of Monarchy and Hereditary Succession

Mankind being originally equals in the order of creation, the equality could only be destroyed by some subsequent circumstance; the distinctions of rich, and poor, may in a great measure be accounted for, and that without having recourse to the harsh, ill-sounding names of oppression and avarice. Oppression is often the consequence, but seldom or never the means of riches; and though avarice will preserve a man from being necessitously poor, it generally makes him too timorous to be wealthy.

But there is another and greater distinction for which no truly natural or religious reason can be assigned, and that is, the distinction of men into KINGS and SUBJECTS. Male and female are the distinctions of nature, good and bad the distinctions of heaven; but how a race of men came into the world so exalted above the rest, and distinguished like some new species, is worth enquiring into, and whether they are the means of happiness or of misery to mankind.

In the early ages of the world, according to the scripture chronology, there were no kings; the consequence of which was there were no wars; it is the pride of kings which throw mankind into confusion. Holland without a king hath enjoyed more peace for this last century than any of the monarchial governments in Europe. Antiquity favors the same remark; for the quiet and rural lives of the first patriarchs hath a happy something in them, which vanishes away when we come to the history of Jewish royalty.

Government by kings was first introduced into the world by the Heathens, from whom the children of Israel copied the custom. It was the most prosperous invention the Devil ever set on foot for the promotion of idolatry. The Heathens paid divine honors to their deceased kings, and the Christian world hath improved on the plan by doing the same to their living ones. How impious is the title of sacred majesty applied to a worm, who in the midst of his splendor is crumbling into dust!

As the exalting one man so greatly above the rest cannot be justified on the equal rights of nature, so neither can it be defended on the authority of scripture; for the will of the Almighty, as declared by Gideon and the prophet Samuel, expressly disapproves of government by kings. All anti-monarchial parts of scripture have been very smoothly glossed over in monarchial governments, but they undoubtedly merit the attention of countries which have their governments yet to form. Render unto Caesar the things which are Caesar's is the scripture doctrine of courts, yet it is no support of monarchial government, for the Jews at that time were without a king, and in a state of vassalage to the Romans.

Near three thousand years passed away from the Mosaic account of the creation, till the Jews under a national delusion requested a king. Till then their form of government (except in extraordinary cases, where the Almighty interposed) was a kind of republic administered by a judge and the elders of the tribes. Kings they had none, and it was held sinful to acknowledge any being under that title but the Lord of Hosts. And when a man seriously reflects on the idolatrous homage which is paid to the persons of kings he need not wonder, that the Almighty, ever jealous of his honor, should disapprove of a form of government which so impiously invades the prerogative of heaven.

Monarchy is ranked in scripture as one of the sins of the Jews, for which a curse in reserve is denounced against them. The history of that transaction is worth attending to.

The children of Israel being oppressed by the Midianites, Gideon marched against them with a small army, and victory, through the divine interposition, decided in his favor. The Jews elate with success, and attributing it to the generalship of Gideon, proposed making him a king, saying, Rule thou over us, thou and thy son and thy son's son. Here was temptation in its fullest extent; not a kingdom only, but an hereditary one, but Gideon in the piety of his soul replied, I will not rule over you, neither shall my son rule over you, THE LORD SHALL RULE OVER YOU. Words need not be more explicit; Gideon doth not decline the honor but denieth their right to give it; neither doth he compliment them with invented declarations of his thanks, but in the positive stile of a prophet charges them with disaffection to their proper Sovereign, the King of heaven.

About one hundred and thirty years after this, they fell again into the same error. The hankering which the Jews had for the idolatrous customs of the Heathens, is something exceedingly unaccountable; but so it was, that laying hold of the misconduct of Samuel's two sons, who were entrusted with some secular concerns, they came in an abrupt and clamorous manner to Samuel, saying, Behold thou art old and thy sons walk not in thy ways, now make us a king to judge us like all other nations. And here we cannot but observe that their motives were bad, viz. that they might be like unto other nations, i.e. the Heathens, whereas their true glory laid in being as much unlike them as possible. But the thing displeased Samuel when they said, give us a king to judge us; and Samuel prayed unto the lord, and the lord said unto Samuel, Hearken unto the voice of the people in all that they say unto thee, for they have not rejected thee, but they have rejected me, THEN I SHOULD NOT REIGN OVER THEM. According to all the works which have done since the day brought them up out of egypt, even unto this day; wherewith they have forsaken me and served other gods; so do they also unto thee. now therefore hearken unto their voice, howbeit, protest solemnly unto them and show them the manner of the king that shall reign over them, i. e., not of any particular king, but the general manner of the kings of the earth, whom Israel was so eagerly copying after. And notwithstanding the great distance of time and difference of manners, the character is still in fashion.

And Samuel told all the words of the Lord unto the people, that asked of him a king. And he said, this shall be the manner of the king that shall reign over you; he will take your sons and appoint them for himself, for his chariots, and to be his horseman, and some shall run before his chariots (this description agrees with the present mode of impressing men) and he will appoint him captains over thousands and captains over fifties, and will set them to ear his ground and to read his harvest, and to make his instruments of war, and instruments of his chariots; and he will take your daughters to be confectionaries and to be cooks and to be bakers (this describes the expense and luxury as well as the oppression of kings) and he will take your fields and your olive yards, even the best of them, and give them to his servants; and he will take the tenth of your seed, and of your vineyards, and give them to his officers and to his servants (by which we see that bribery, corruption, and favouritism are the standing vices of kings) and he will take the tenth of your men servants, and your maid servants, and your goodliest young men and your asses, and put them to his word; and he will take the tenth of your sheep, and ye shall be his servants, and ye shall cry out in that day because of your king which ye shall have chosen, AND THE LORD WILL NOT HEAR YOU IN THAT DAY. This accounts for the continuation of monarchy; neither do the characters of the few good kings which have lived since, either sanctify the title, or blot out the sinfulness of the origin; the high encomium given of David takes no notice of him officially as a king, but only as a man after God's own heart. Nevertheless the people refused to obey the voice of Samuel, and they said, Nay, but we will have a king over us, that we may be like all the nations, and that our king may judge us, and go out before us, and fight our battles. Samuel continued to reason with them, but to no purpose; he set before them their ingratitude, but all would not avail; and seeing them fully bent on their folly, he cried out, I will call unto the Lord, and he shall send thunder and rain (which then was a punishment, being in the time of wheat harvest) that ye may perceive and see that your wickedness is great which ye have done in the sight of the Lord, IN ASKING YOU A KING. So Samuel called unto the Lord, and the Lord sent thunder and rain that day, and all the people greatly feared the Lord and Samuel. And all the people said unto Samuel, Pray for thy servants unto the Lord thy God that we die not, for WE HAVE ADDED UNTO OUR SINS THIS EVIL, TO ASK A KING. These portions of scripture are direct and positive. They admit of no equivocal construction.

That the Almighty hath here entered his protest against monarchical government, is true, or the scripture is false. And a man hath good reason to believe that there is as much of kingcraft, as priestcraft in withholding the scripture from the public in Popish countries. For monarchy in every instance is the Popery of government.

To the evil of monarchy we have added that of hereditary succession; and as the first is a degradation and lessening of ourselves, so the second, claimed as a matter of right, is an insult and an imposition on posterity. For all men being originally equals, no one by birth could have a right to set up his own family in perpetual preference to all others for ever, and though himself might deserve some decent degree of honours of his contemporaries, yet his descendants might be far too unworthy to inherit them. One of the strongest natural proofs of the folly of hereditary right in kings, is, that nature disapproves it, otherwise she would not so frequently turn it into ridicule by giving mankind an ass for a lion.

Secondly, as no man at first could possess any other public honours than were bestowed upon him, so the givers of those honours could have no power to give away the right of posterity. And though they might say, "we choose you for our head," they could not, without manifest injustice to their children, say, "that your children and your children's children shall reign over ours for ever." Because such an unwise, unjust, unnatural compact might (perhaps) in the next succession put them under the government of a rogue or a fool. Most wise men, in their private sentiments, have ever treated hereditary right with contempt; yet it is one of those evils, which when once established is not easily removed; many submit from fear, others from superstition, and the more powerful part shares with the king the plunder of the rest.

This is supposing the present race of kings in the world to have had an honourable origin; whereas it is more than probable, that could we take off the dark covering of antiquity, and trace them to their first rise, that we should find the first of them nothing better than the principal ruffian of some restless gang, whose savage manners of preeminence in subtlety obtained him the title of chief among plunderers; and who by increasing in power, and extending his depredations, overawed the quiet and defenseless to purchase their safety by frequent contributions. Yet his electors could have no idea of giving hereditary right to his descendants, because such a perpetual exclusion of themselves was incompatible with the free and unrestrained principles they professed to live by. Wherefore, hereditary succession in the early ages of monarchy could not take place as a matter of claim, but as something casual or complemental; but as few or no records were extant in those days, and traditionary history stuffed with fables, it was very easy, after the lapse of a few generations, to trump up some superstitious tale, conveniently timed, Mahomet like, to cram hereditary right down the throats of the vulgar. Perhaps the disorders which threatened, or seemed to threaten on the decease of a leader and the choice of a new one (for elections among ruffians could not be very orderly) induced many at first to favor hereditary pretensions; by which means it happened, as it hath happened since, that what at first was submitted to as a convenience, was afterwards claimed as a right.

England, since the conquest, hath known some few good monarchs, but groaned beneath a much larger number of bad ones; yet no man in his senses can say that their claim under William the Conqueror is a very honourable one. A French bastard landing with an armed banditti, and establishing himself king of England against the consent of the natives, is in plain terms a very paltry rascally original. It certainly hath no divinity in it. However, it is needless to spend much time in exposing the folly of hereditary right; if there are any so weak as to believe it, let them promiscuously worship the ass and lion, and welcome. I shall neither copy their humility, nor disturb their devotion.

Yet I should be glad to ask how they suppose kings came at first? The question admits but of three answers, viz. either by lot, by election, or by usurpation.

If the first king was taken by lot, it establishes a precedent for the next, which excludes hereditary succession. Saul was by lot, yet the succession was not hereditary, neither does it appear from that transaction there was any intention it ever should be. If the first king of any country was by election, that likewise establishes a precedent for the next; for to say, that the right of all future generations is taken away, by the act of the first electors, in their choice not only of a king, but of a family of kings for ever, hath no parallel in or out of scripture but the doctrine of original sin, which supposes the free will of all men lost in Adam; and from such comparison, and it will admit of no other, hereditary succession can derive no glory. For as in Adam all sinned, and as in the first electors all men obeyed; as in the one all mankind were subjected to Satan, and in the other to Sovereignty; as our innocence was lost in the first, and our authority in the last; and as both disable us from reassuming some former state and privilege, it unanswerably follows that original sin and hereditary succession are parallels. Dishonourable rank! Inglorious connection! Yet the most subtle sophist cannot produce a juster simile.

As to usurpation, no man will be so hardy as to defend it; and that William the Conqueror was an usurper is a fact not to be contradicted. The plain truth is, that the antiquity of English monarchy will not bear looking into.

But it is not so much the absurdity as the evil of hereditary succession which concerns mankind. Did it ensure a race of good and wise men it would have the seal of divine authority, but as it opens a door to the foolish, the wicked, and the improper, it hath in it the nature of oppression. Men who look upon themselves born to reign, and others to obey, soon grow insolent; selected from the rest of mankind their minds are early poisoned by importance; and the world they act in differs so materially from the world at large, that they have but little opportunity of knowing its true interests, and when they succeed to the government are frequently the most ignorant and unfit of any throughout the dominions.

Another evil which attends hereditary succession is, that the throne is subject to be possessed by a minor at any age; all which time the regency, acting under the cover of a king, have every opportunity and inducement to betray their trust.

The same national misfortune happens, when a king worn out with age and infirmity, enters the last stage of human weakness. In both these cases the public becomes a prey to every miscreant, who can tamper successfully with the follies either of age or infancy.

The most plausible plea, which hath ever been offered in favor of hereditary succession, is, that it preserves a nation from civil wars; and were this true, it would be weighty; whereas, it is the most barefaced falsity ever imposed upon mankind. The whole history of England disowns the fact. Thirty kings and two minors have reigned in that distracted kingdom since the conquest, in which time there have been (including the Revolution) no less than eight civil wars and nineteen rebellions. Wherefore instead of making for peace, it makes against it, and destroys the very foundation it seems to stand on.

The contest for monarchy and succession, between the houses of York and Lancaster, laid England in a scene of blood for many years. Twelve pitched battles, besides skirmishes and sieges, were fought between Henry and Edward.

Twice was Henry prisoner to Edward, who in his turn was prisoner to Henry. And so uncertain is the fate of war and the temper of a nation, when nothing but personal matters are the ground of a quarrel, that Henry was taken in triumph from a prison to a palace, and Edward obliged to fly from a palace to a foreign land; yet, as sudden transitions of temper are seldom lasting, Henry in his turn was driven from the throne, and Edward recalled to succeed him. The parliament always following the strongest side.

This contest began in the reign of Henry the Sixth, and was not entirely extinguished till Henry the Seventh, in whom the families were united. Including a period of 67 years, viz. from 1422 to 1489.

In short, monarchy and succession have laid (not this or that kingdom only) but the world in blood and ashes. 'Tis a form of government which the word of God bears testimony against, and blood will attend it.

If we inquire into the business of a king, we shall find that in some countries they have none; and after sauntering away their lives without pleasure to themselves or advantage to the nation, withdraw from the scene, and leave their successors to tread the same idle round. In absolute monarchies the whole weight of business civil and military, lies on the king; the children of Israel in their request for a king, urged this plea "that he may judge us, and go out before us and fight our battles." But in countries where he is neither a judge nor a general, as in England, a man would be puzzled to know what is his business.

The nearer any government approaches to a republic, the less business there is for a king. It is somewhat difficult to find a proper name for the government of England. Sir William Meredith calls it a republic; but in its present state it is unworthy of the name, because the corrupt influence of the crown, by having all the places in its disposal, hath so effectually swallowed up the power, and eaten out the virtue of the house of commons (the republican part in the constitution) that the government of England is nearly as monarchical as that of France or Spain.

Men fall out with names without understanding them. For it is the republican and not the monarchical part of the constitution of England which Englishmen glory in, viz. the liberty of choosing a house of commons from out of their own body and it is easy to see that when the republican virtue fails, slavery ensues. Why is the constitution of England sickly, but because monarchy hath poisoned the republic, the crown hath engrossed the commons?

In England a king hath little more to do than to make war and give away places; which in plain terms, is to impoverish the nation and set it together by the ears. A pretty business indeed for a man to be allowed eight hundred thousand sterling a year for, and worshipped into the bargain! Of more worth is one honest man to society and in the sight of God, than all the crowned ruffians that ever lived.

Thoughts of the Present State of American Affairs

In the following pages I offer nothing more than simple facts, plain arguments, and common sense; and have no other Preliminaries to settle with the reader, than that he will divest himself of prejudice and prepossession, and suffer his reason and his feelings to determine for themselves; that he will put on, or rather that he will not put off the true character of a man, and generously enlarge his views beyond the present day.

Volumes have been written on the subject of the struggle between England and America. Men of all ranks have embarked in the controversy, from different motives, and with various designs; but all have been ineffectual, and the period of debate is closed. Arms, as the last resource, decide the contest; the appeal was the choice of the king, and the continent hath accepted the challenge.

It hath been reported of the late Mr. Pelham (who tho' an able minister was not without his faults) that on his being attacked in the house of commons, on the score, that his measures were only of a temporary kind, replied, "they will fast my time." Should a thought so fatal and unmanly possess the colonies in the present contest, the name of ancestors will be remembered by future generations with detestation.

The sun never shined on a cause of greater worth. 'Tis not the affair of a city, a county, a province, or a kingdom, but of a continent—of at least one eighth part of the habitable globe. 'Tis not the concern of a day, a year, or an age; posterity are virtually involved in the contest, and will be more or less affected, even to the end of time, by the proceedings now. Now is the seed time of continental union, faith and honour. The least fracture now will be like a name engraved with the point of a pin on the tender rind of a young oak; the wound will enlarge with the tree, and posterity read it in full grown characters.

By referring the matter from argument to arms, a new area for politics is struck; a new method of thinking hath arisen. All plans, proposals, &c. prior to the nineteenth of April, i. e., to the commencement of hostilities, are like the almanacs of the last year;

which, though proper then are superseded and useless now. Whatever was advanced by the advocates on either side of the question then, terminated in one and the same point. viz. a union with Great Britain: the only difference between the parties was the method of effecting it; the one proposing force, the other friendship; but it hath so far happened that the first hath failed, and the second hath withdrawn her influence.

As much hath been said of the advantages of reconciliation which, like an agreeable dream, hath passed away and left us as we were, it is but right, that we should examine the contrary side of the argument, and inquire into some of the many material injuries which these colonies sustain, and always will sustain, by being connected with, and dependant on Great Britain: To examine that connection and dependance, on the principles of nature and common sense, to see what we have to trust to, if separated, and what we are to expect, if dependant.

I have heard it asserted by some, that as America hath flourished under her former connection with Great Britain that the same connection is necessary towards her future happiness, and will always have the same effect. Nothing can be more fallacious than this kind of argument. We may as well assert that because a child has thrived upon milk that it is never to have meat, or that the first twenty years of our lives is to become a precedent for the next twenty. But even this is admitting more than is true, for I answer roundly, that America would have flourished as much, and probably much more, had no European power had any thing to do with her. The commerce, by which she hath enriched herself, are the necessaries of life, and will always have a market while eating is the custom of Europe.

But she has protected us, say some. That she hath engrossed us is true, and defended the continent at our expense as well as her own is admitted, and she would have defended Turkey from the same motive, viz. the sake of trade and dominion.

Alas, we have been long led away by ancient prejudices, and made large sacrifices to superstition. We have boasted the protection of Great Britain, without considering, that her motive was interest not attachment; that she did not protect us from our enemies on our account, but from her enemies on her own account, from those who had no quarrel with us on any other account, and who will always be our enemies on the same account. Let Britain wave her pretensions to the continent, or the continent throw off the dependance, and we should be at peace with France and Spain were they at war with Britain. The miseries of Hanover last war ought to warn us against connections.

It hath lately been asserted in parliament, that the colonies have no relation to each other but through the parent country, i. e. that Pennsylvania and the Jerseys, and so on for the rest, are sister colonies by the way of England; this is certainly a very roundabout way of proving relationship, but it is the nearest and only true way of proving enemyship, if I may so call it. France and Spain never were, nor perhaps ever will be our enemies as Americans, but as our being the subjects of Great Britain.

But Britain is the parent country, say some. Then the more shame upon her conduct. Even brutes do not devour their young, nor savages make war upon their families; wherefore the assertion, if true, turns to her reproach; but it happens not to be true, or only partly so and the phrase parent or mother country hath been jesuitically adopted by the king and his parasites, with a low papistical design of gaining an unfair bias on the credulous weakness of our minds. Europe, and not England, is the parent country of America. This new world hath been the asylum for the persecuted lovers of civil and religious liberty from every part of Europe.

Hither have they fled, not from the tender embraces of the mother, but from the cruelty of the monster; and it is so far true of England, that the same tyranny which drove the first emigrants from home pursues their descendants still.

In this extensive quarter of the globe, we forget the narrow limits of three hundred and sixty miles (the extent of England) and carry our friendship on a larger scale; we claim brotherhood with every European Christian, and triumph in the generosity of the sentiment.

It is pleasant to observe by what regular gradations we surmount the force of local prejudice, as we enlarge our acquaintance with the world. A man born in any town in England divided into parishes, will naturally associate most with his fellow parishioners (because their interests in many cases will be common) and distinguish him by the name of neighbour; if he meet him but a few miles from home, he drops the narrow idea of a street, and salutes him by the name of townsman; if he travels out of the county, and meet him in any other, he forgets the minor divisions of street and town, and calls him countryman, i. e., countyman; but if in their foreign excursions they should associate in France or any other part of Europe, their local remembrance would be enlarged into that of Englishmen. And by a just parity of reasoning, all Europeans meeting in America, or any other quarter of the globe, are countrymen; for England, Holland, Germany, or Sweden, when compared with the whole, stand in the same places on the larger scale, which the divisions of street, town, and county do on the smaller ones; distinctions too limited for continental minds. Not one third of the inhabitants, even of this province, are of English descent. Wherefore I reprobate the phrase of parent or mother country applied to England only, as being false, selfish, narrow and ungenerous.

But admitting that we were all of English descent, what does it amount to? Nothing. Britain, being now an open enemy, extinguishes every other name and title: And to say that reconciliation is our duty, is truly farcical. The first king of England, of the present line (William the Conqueror) was a Frenchman, and half the Peers of England are descendants from the same country; wherefore by the same method of reasoning, England ought to be governed by France.

Much hath been said of the united strength of Britain and the colonies, that in conjunction they might bid defiance to the world. But this is mere presumption; the fate of war is uncertain, neither do the expressions mean anything; for this continent would never suffer itself to be drained of inhabitants to support the British arms in either Asia, Africa, or Europe.

Besides, what have we to do with setting the world at defiance? Our plan is commerce, and that, well attended to, will secure us the peace and friendship of all Europe; because, it is the interest of all Europe to have America a free port. Her trade will always be a protection, and her barrenness of gold and silver secure her from invaders.

I challenge the warmest advocate for reconciliation, to show, a single advantage that this continent can reap, by being connected with Great Britain. I repeat the challenge, not a single advantage is derived. Our corn will fetch its price in any market in Europe, and our imported goods must be paid for buy them where we will.

But the injuries and disadvantages we sustain by that connection, are without number; and our duty to mankind at large, as well as to ourselves, instruct us to renounce the alliance: Because, any submission to, or dependance on Great Britain, tends directly to involve this continent in European wars and quarrels; and sets us at variance with nations, who would otherwise seek our friendship, and against whom, we have neither anger nor complaint. As Europe is our market for trade, we ought to form no partial connection with any part of it. It is the true interest of America to steer clear of European contentions, which she never can do, while by her dependance on Britain, she is made the make-weight in the scale of British politics.

Europe is too thickly planted with kingdoms to be long at peace, and whenever a war breaks out between England and any foreign power, the trade of America goes to ruin, because of her connection with Britain. The next war may not turn out like the last, and should it not, the advocates for reconciliation now, will be wishing for separation then, because, neutrality in that case, would be a safer convoy than a man of war. Every thing that is right or natural pleads for separation. The blood of the slain, the weeping voice of nature cries, 'tis time to part.

Even the distance at which the Almighty hath placed England and America, is a strong and natural proof, that the authority of the one, over the other, was never the design of Heaven. The time likewise at which the continent was discovered, adds weight to the argument, and the manner in which it was peopled increases the force of it. The reformation was preceded by the discovery of America, as if the Almighty graciously meant to open a sanctuary to the persecuted in future years, when home should afford neither friendship nor safety.

The authority of Great Britain over this continent, is a form of government, which sooner or later must have an end: And a serious mind can draw no true pleasure by looking forward, under the painful and positive conviction, that what he calls "the present constitution" is merely temporary. As parents, we can have no joy, knowing that this government is not sufficiently lasting to ensure any thing which we may bequeath to posterity: And by a plain method of argument, as we are running the next generation into debt, we ought to do the work of it, otherwise we use them meanly and pitifully. In order to discover the line of our duty rightly, we should take our children in our hand, and fix our station a few years farther into life; that eminence will present a prospect, which a few present fears and prejudices conceal from our sight.

Though I would carefully avoid giving unnecessary offence, yet I am inclined to believe, that all those who espouse the doctrine of reconciliation, may be included within the following descriptions. Interested men, who are not to be trusted; weak men, who cannot see; prejudiced men, who will not see; and a certain set of moderate men, who think better of the European world than it deserves; and this last class by an ill-judged deliberation, will be the cause of more calamities to this continent, than all the other three.

It is the good fortune of many to live distant from the scene of sorrow; the evil is not sufficiently brought to their doors to make them feel the precariousness with which all American property is possessed. But let our imaginations transport us for a few moments to Boston, that seat of wretchedness will teach us wisdom, and instruct us for ever to renounce a power in whom we can have no trust. The inhabitants of that unfortunate city, who but a few months ago were in ease and affluence, have now no other alternative than to stay and starve, or turn out to beg. Endangered by the fire of their friends if they continue within the city, and plundered by the soldiery if they leave it. In their present condition they are prisoners without the hope of redemption, and in a general attack for their relief, they would be exposed to the fury of both armies.

Men of passive tempers look somewhat lightly over the offenses of Britain, and, still hoping for the best, are apt to call out, Come we shall be friends again for all this. But examine the passions and feelings of mankind. Bring the doctrine of reconciliation to the touchstone of nature, and then tell me, whether you can hereafter love, honor, and faithfully serve the power that hath carried fire and sword into your land? If you cannot do all these, then are you only deceiving yourselves, and by your delay bringing ruin upon posterity. Your future connection with Britain, whom you can neither love nor honor, will be forced and unnatural, and being formed only on the plan of present convenience, will in a little time fall into a relapse more wretched than the first. But if you say, you can still pass the violations over, then I ask, Hath your house been burnt? Hath your property been destroyed before your face? Are your wife and children destitute of a bed to lie on, or bread to live on? Have you lost a parent or a child by their hands, and yourself the ruined and wretched survivor? If you have not, then are you not a judge of those who have. But if you have, and can still shake hands with the murderers, then are you unworthy of the name of husband, father, friend, or lover, and whatever may be your rank or title in life, you have the heart of a coward, and the spirit of a sycophant.

This is not inflaming or exaggerating matters, but trying them by those feelings and affections which nature justifies, and without which, we should be incapable of discharging the social duties of life, or enjoying the felicities of it. I mean not to exhibit horror for the purpose of provoking revenge, but to awaken us from fatal and unmanly slumbers, that we may pursue determinately some fixed object. It is not in the power of Britain or of Europe to conquer America, if she do not conquer herself by delay and timidity. The present winter is worth an age if rightly employed, but if lost or neglected, the whole continent will partake of the misfortune; and there is no punishment which that man will not deserve, be he who, or what, or where he will, that may be the means of sacrificing a season so precious and useful.

It is repugnant to reason, to the universal order of things, to all examples from the former ages, to suppose, that this continent can longer remain subject to any external power. The most sanguine in Britain does not think so. The utmost stretch of human wisdom cannot, at this time, compass a plan short of separation, which can promise the continent even a year's security. Reconciliation is and was a fallacious dream. Nature hath deserted the connection, and Art cannot supply her place. For, as Milton wisely expresses, "never can true reconcilement grow where wounds of deadly hate have pierced so deep."Every quiet method for peace hath been ineffectual. Our prayers have been rejected with disdain; and only tended to convince us, that nothing flatters vanity, or confirms obstinacy in Kings more than repeated petitioning and nothing hath contributed more than that very measure to make the Kings of Europe absolute: Witness Denmark and Sweden. Wherefore, since nothing but blows will do, for God's sake, let us come to a final separation, and not leave the next generation to be cutting throats, under the violated unmeaning names of parent and child.

To say, they will never attempt it again is idle and visionary, we thought so at the repeal of the stamp act, yet a year or two undeceived us; as well we may suppose that nations, which have been once defeated, will never renew the quarrel.

As to government matters, it is not in the powers of Britain to do this continent justice: The business of it will soon be too weighty, and intricate, to be managed with any tolerable degree of convenience, by a power, so distant from us, and so very ignorant of us; for if they cannot conquer us, they cannot govern us. To be always running three or four thousand miles with a tale or a petition, waiting four or five months for an answer, which when obtained requires five or six more to explain it in, will in a few years be looked upon as folly and childishness, there was a time when it was proper, and there is a proper time for it to cease.

Small islands not capable of protecting themselves, are the proper objects for kingdoms to take under their care; but there is something very absurd, in supposing a continent to be perpetually governed by an island. In no instance hath nature made the satellite larger than its primary planet, and as England and America, with respect to each other, reverses the common order of nature, it is evident they belong to different systems: England to Europe, America to itself.

I am not induced by motives of pride, party, or resentment to espouse the doctrine of separation and independance; I am clearly, positively, and conscientiously persuaded that it is the true interest of this continent to be so; that every thing short of that is mere patchwork, that it can afford no lasting felicity, that it is leaving the sword to our children, and shrinking back at a time, when, a little more, a little farther, would have rendered this continent the glory of the earth.

As Britain hath not manifested the least inclination towards a compromise, we may be assured that no terms can be obtained worthy the acceptance of the continent, or any ways equal to the expense of blood and treasure we have been already put to.

The object contended for, ought always to bear some just proportion to the expense. The removal of the North, or the whole detestable junto, is a matter unworthy the millions we have expended. A temporary stoppage of trade, was an inconvenience, which would have sufficiently balanced the repeal of all the acts complained of, had such repeals been obtained; but if the whole continent must take up arms, if every man must be a soldier, it is scarcely worth our while to fight against a contemptible ministry only. Dearly, dearly, do we pay for the repeal of the acts, if that is all we fight for; for in a just estimation, it is as great a folly to pay a Bunker Hill price for law, as for land. As I have always considered the independancy of this continent, as an event, which sooner or later must arrive, so from the late rapid progress of the continent to maturity, the event could not be far off. Wherefore, on the breaking out of hostilities, it was not worth the while to have disputed a matter, which time would have finally redressed, unless we meant to be in earnest; otherwise, it is like wasting an estate of a suit at law, to regulate the trespasses of a tenant, whose lease is just expiring. No man was a warmer wisher for reconciliation than myself, before the fatal nineteenth of April 1775 (Massacre at Lexington), but the moment the event of that day was made known, I rejected the hardened, sullen tempered Pharaoh of England for ever; and disdain the wretch, that with the pretended title of father of his people, can unfeelingly hear of their slaughter, and composedly sleep with their blood upon his soul.

But admitting that matters were now made up, what would be the event? I answer, the ruin of the continent. And that for several reasons: First. The powers of governing still remaining in the hands of the king, he will have a negative over the whole legislation of this continent. And as he hath shown himself such an inveterate enemy to liberty, and discovered such a thirst for arbitrary power; is he, or is he not, a proper man to say to these colonies, "you shall make no laws but what I please." And is there any inhabitant in America so ignorant as not to know, that according to what is called the present constitution, that this continent can make no laws but what the king gives leave to; and is there any man so unwise, as not to see, that (considering what has happened) he will suffer no law to be made here, but such as suit his purpose. We may be as effectually enslaved by the want of laws in America, as by submitting to laws made for us in England. After matters are made up (as it is called) can there be any doubt, but the whole power of the crown will be exerted, to keep this continent as low and humble as possible? Instead of going forward we shall go backward, or be perpetually quarrelling or ridiculously petitioning. We are already greater than the king wishes us to be, and will he not hereafter endeavour to make us less? To bring the matter to one point. Is the power who is jealous of our prosperity, a proper power to govern us? Whoever says No to this question, is an independant, for independancy means no more, than, whether we shall make our own laws, or whether the king, the greatest enemy this continent hath, or can have, shall tell us, "there shall be now laws but such as I like."

But the king you will say has a negative in England; the people there can make no laws without his consent. In point of right and good order, there is something very ridiculous, that a youth of twenty-one (which hath often happened) shall say to several millions of people, older and wiser than himself, I forbid this or that act of yours to be law. But in this place I decline this sort of reply, though I will never cease to expose the absurdity of it, and only answer, that England being the

King's residence, and America not so, makes quite another case. The king's negative here is ten times more dangerous and fatal than it can be in England, for there he will scarcely refuse his consent to a bill for putting England into as strong a state of defence as possible, and in America he would never suffer such a bill to be passed.

America is only a secondary object in the system of British politics, England consults the good of this country, no farther than it answers her own purpose.

Wherefore, her own interest leads her to suppress the growth of ours in every case which doth not promote her advantage, or in the least interfere with it. A pretty state we should soon be in under such a secondhand government, considering what has happened! Men do not change from enemies to friends by the alteration of a name: And in order to show that reconciliation now is a dangerous doctrine, I affirm, that it would be policy in the kingdom at this time, to repeal the acts for the sake of reinstating himself in the government of the provinces; in order, that he may accomplish by craft and subtlety, in the long run, what he cannot do by force and violence in the short one. Reconciliation and ruin are nearly related.

Secondly. That as even the best terms, which we can expect to obtain, can amount to no more than a temporary expedient, or a kind of government by guardianship, which can last no longer than till the colonies come of age, so the general face and state of things, in the interim, will be unsettled and unpromising. Emigrants of property will not choose to come to a country whose form of government hangs but by a thread, and who is every day tottering on the brink of commotion and disturbance; and numbers of the present inhabitants would lay hold of the interval, to dispense of their effects, and quit the continent.

But the most powerful of all arguments, is, that nothing but independance, i.e. a continental form of government, can keep the peace of the continent and preserve it inviolate from civil wars. I dread the event of a reconciliation with Britain now, as it is more than probable, that it will be followed by a revolt somewhere or other, the consequences of which may be far more fatal than all the malice of Britain.

Thousands are already ruined by British barbarity; (thousands more will probably suffer the same fate.) Those men have other feelings than us who have nothing suffered. All they now possess is liberty, what they before enjoyed is sacrificed to its service, and having nothing more to lose, they disdain submission. Besides, the general temper of the colonies, towards a British government, will be like that of a youth, who is nearly out of his time; they will care very little about her. And a government which cannot preserve the peace, is no government at all, and in that case we pay our money for nothing; and pray what is it that Britain can do, whose power will be wholly on paper, should a civil tumult break out the very day after reconciliation? I have heard some men say, many of whom I believe spoke without thinking, that they dreaded an independance, fearing that it would produce civil wars. It is but seldom that our first thoughts are truly correct, and that is the case here; for there are ten times more to dread from a patched up connection than from independznce. I make the sufferers case my own, and I protest, that were I driven from house and home, my property destroyed, and my circumstances ruined, that as man, sensible of injuries, I could never relish the doctrine of reconciliation, or consider myself bound thereby.

The colonies have manifested such a spirit of good order and obedience to continental government, as is sufficient to make every reasonable person easy and happy on that head. No man can assign the least pretence for his fears, on any other grounds, that such as are truly childish and ridiculous, viz. that one colony will be striving for superiority over another.

Where there are no distinctions there can be no superiority, perfect equality affords no temptation. The republics of Europe are all (and we may say always) in peace. Holland and Switzerland are without wars, foreign or domestic; monarchical governments, it is true, are never long at rest; the crown itself is a temptation to enterprising ruffians at home; and that degree of pride and insolence ever attendant on regal authority, swells into a rupture with foreign powers, in instances where a republican government, by being formed on more natural principles, would negotiate the mistake.

If there is any true cause of fear respecting independance it is because no plan is yet laid down. Men do not see their way out; Wherefore, as an opening into that business, I offer the following hints; at the same time modestly affirming, that I have no other opinion of them myself, than that they may be the means of giving rise to something better. Could the straggling thoughts of individuals be collected, they would frequently form materials for wise and able men to improve to useful matter.

Let the assemblies be annual, with a President only. The representation more equal. Their business wholly domestic, and subject to the authority of a Continental Congress.

Let each colony be divided into six, eight, or ten, convenient districts, each district to send a proper number of delegates to Congress, so that each colony send at least thirty. The whole number in Congress will be at least three hundred ninety.

Each Congress to sit··· and to choose a president by the following method. When the delegates are met, let a colony be taken from the whole thirteen colonies by lot, after which let the whole Congress choose (by ballot) a president from out of the delegates of that province. In the next Congress, let a colony be taken by lot from twelve only, omitting that colony from which the president was taken in the former Congress, and so proceeding on till the whole thirteen shall have had their proper rotation. And in order that nothing may pass into a law but what is satisfactorily just, not less than three fifths of the Congress to be called a majority. He that will promote discord, under a government so equally formed as this, would join Lucifer in his revolt.

But as there is a peculiar delicacy, from whom, or in what manner, this business must first arise, and as it seems most agreeable and consistent, that it should come from some intermediate body between the governed and the governors, that is between the Congress and the people. Let a Continental Conference be held, in the following manner, and for the following purpose: A committee of twenty-six members of Congress, viz. two for each colony.

Two members for each house of assembly, or provincial

convention; and five representatives of the people at large, to be chosen in the capital city or town of each province, for, and in behalf of the whole province, by as many qualified voters as shall think proper to attend from all parts of the province for that purpose; or, if more convenient, the representatives may be chosen in two or three of the most populous parts thereof. In this conference, thus assembled, will be united, the two grand principles of business knowledge and power. The members of Congress, Assemblies, or Conventions, by having had experience in national concerns, will be able and useful counsellors, and the whole, being empowered by the people will have a truly legal authority.

The conferring members being met, let their business be to frame a Continental Charter, or Charter of the United Colonies; (answering to what is called the Magna Charta of England) fixing the number and manner of choosing members of Congress, members of Assembly, with their date of sitting, and drawing the line of business and jurisdiction between them: always remembering, that our strength is continental, not provincial: Securing freedom and property to all men, and above all things the free exercise of religion, according to the dictates of conscience; with such other matter as is necessary for a charter to contain. Immediately after which, the said Conference to dissolve, and the bodies which shall be chosen comformable to the said charter, to be the legislators and governors of this continent for the time being: Whose peace and happiness, may God preserve, Amen.

Should any body of men be hereafter delegated for this or some similar purpose, I offer them the following extracts from that wise observer on governments Dragonetti. "The science" says he "of the politician consists in fixing the true point of happiness and freedom. Those men would deserve the gratitude of ages, who should discover a mode of government that contained the greatest sum of individual happiness, with the least national expense." [1]

But where says some is the King of America? I'll tell you Friend, he reigns above, and doth not make havoc of mankind like the Royal of Britain. Yet that we may not appear to be defective even in earthly honors, let a day be solemnly set apart for proclaiming the charter; let it be brought forth placed on the divine law, the word of God; let a crown be placed thereon, by which the world may know, that so far as we approve of monarchy, that in America the law is king. For as in absolute governments the King is law, so in free countries the law ought to be King; and there ought to be no other. But lest any

---

[1]   Dragonetti on Virtue and Rewards.

ill use should afterwards arise, let the crown at the conclusion of the ceremony be demolished, and scattered among the people whose right it is.

A government of our own is our natural right: And when a man seriously reflects on the precariousness of human affairs, he will become convinced, that it is infinitely wiser and safer, to form a constitution of our own in a cool deliberate manner, while we have it in our power, than to trust such an interesting event to time and chance. If we omit it now, some Massanello [1] may hereafter arise, who laying hold of popular disquietudes, may collect together the desperate and the discontented, and by assuming to themselves the powers of government, may sweep away the liberties of the continent like a deluge. Should the government of America return again into the hands of Britain, the tottering situation of things, will be a temptation for some desperate adventurer to try his fortune; and in such a case, what relief can Britain give? Ere she could hear the news the fatal business might be done; and ourselves suffering like the wretched Britons under

---

[1] Thomas Anello, otherwise Massenello, a fishman of Naples, who after spiriting up his countrymen in the public market place, against the oppression of the Spaniards, to whom the place was then subject, prompted them to revolt, and in the space of a day became King.

the oppression of the Conqueror. Ye that oppose independence now, ye know not what ye do; ye are opening a door to eternal tyranny, by keeping vacant the seat of government.

There are thousands and tens of thousands, who would think it glorious to expel from the continent, that barbarous and hellish power, which hath stirred up the Indians and Negroes to destroy us; the cruelty hath a double guilt, it is dealing brutally by us, and treacherously by them. To talk of friendship with those in whom our reason forbids us to have faith, and our affections, (wounded through a thousand pores) instruct us to detest, is madness and folly. Every day wears out the little remains of kindred between us and them, and can there be any reason to hope, that as the relationship expires, the affection will increase, or that we shall agree better, when we have ten times more and greater concerns to quarrel over than ever?

Ye that tell us of harmony and reconciliation, can ye restore to us the time that is past? Can ye give to prostitution its former innocence? Neither can ye reconcile Britain and America. The last cord now is broken, the people of England are presenting addresses against us. There are injuries which nature cannot forgive; she would cease to be nature if she did. As well can the lover forgive the ravisher of his mistress, as the continent forgive the murders of Britain. The Almighty hath implanted in us these inextinguishable feelings for good and wise purposes. They are the guardians of his image in our hearts. They distinguish us from the herd of common animals. The social compact would dissolve, and justice be extirpated the earth, or have only a casual existence were we callous to the touches of affection. The robber, and the murderer, would often escape unpunished, did not the injuries which our tempers sustain, provoke us into justice.

O ye that love mankind! Ye that dare oppose, not only the tyranny, but the tyrant, stand forth! Every spot of the old world is overrun with oppression. Freedom hath been hunted round the globe. Asia, and Africa, have long expelled her. Europe regards her like a stranger, and England hath given her warning to depart. O! receive the fugitive, and prepare in time an asylum for mankind.

Of the Present Ability of America, with Some Miscellaneous Reflections

I HAVE never met with a man, either in England or America, who hath not confessed his opinion that a separation between the countries, would take place one time or other. And there is no instance in which vile have shown less judgement, than in endeavouring to describe, what we call, the ripeness or fitness of the Continent for independance.

As all men allow the measure, and vary only in their opinion of the time, let us, in order to remove mistakes, take a general survey of things, and endeavour if possible, to find out the very time. But we need not go far, the inquiry ceases at once, for the time hath found us. The general concurrence, the glorious union of all things prove the fact.

It is not in numbers but in unity, that our great strength lies; yet our present numbers are sufficient to repel the force of all the world. The Continent hath, at this time, the largest body of armed and disciplined men of any power under Heaven; and is just arrived at that pitch of strength, in which no single colony is able to support itself, and the whole, when united can accomplish the matter, and either more, or, less than this, might be fatal in its effects. Our land force is already sufficient, and as to naval affairs, we cannot be insensible, that Britain would never suffer an American man of war to be built while the continent remained in her hands. Wherefore we should be no forwarder an hundred years hence in that branch, than we are now; but the truth is, we should be less so, because the timber of the country is every day diminishing, and that which will remain at last, will be far off and difficult to procure.

Were the continent crowded with inhabitants, her sufferings under the present circumstances would be intolerable. The more sea port towns we had, the more should we have both to defend and to loose. Our present numbers are so happily proportioned to our wants, that no man need be idle. The diminution of trade affords an army, and the necessities of an army create a new trade. Debts we have none; and whatever we may contract on this account will serve as a glorious memento of our virtue. Can we but leave posterity with a settled form of government, an independant constitution of its own, the purchase at any price will be cheap. But to expend millions for the sake of getting a few vile acts repealed, and routing the present ministry only, is unworthy the charge, and is using posterity with the utmost cruelty; because it is leaving them the great work to do, and a debt upon their backs, from which they derive no advantage. Such a thought is unworthy of a man of honor, and is the true characteristic of a narrow heart and a peddling politician.

The debt we may contract doth not deserve our regard if the work be but accomplished. No nation ought to be without a debt. A national debt is a national bond; and when it bears no interest, is in no case a grievance. Britain is oppressed with a debt of upwards of one hundred and forty millions sterling, for which she pays upwards of four millions interest. And as a compensation for her debt, she has a large navy; America is without a debt, and without a navy; yet for the twentieth part of the English national debt, could have a navy as large again. The navy of England is not worth, at this time, more than three millions and an half sterling.

The first and second editions of this pamphlet were published without the following calculations, which are now given as a proof that the above estimation of the navy is a just one. [1]

The charge of building a ship of each rate, and furnishing her with masts, yards, sails and rigging, together with a proportion of eight months boatswain's and carpenter's seastores, as calculated by Mr. Burchett, Secretary to the navy, is as follows:

For a ship of 100 guns	pounds Sterling-35,553
90	29,886
80	23,638
70	17,785
60	14,197
50	10,606
40	7,558
30	5,846
20	3,710

And from hence it is easy to sum up the value, or cost rather, of the whole British navy, which in the year 1757, when it was at its greatest glory consisted of the following ships and guns:

---

[1] See Entic's naval history, intro. page 56.

Ships.	Guns.	Cost of one	Cost of all
6	100	35,553	213,318
12	90	29,886	358,632
12	80	23,638	283,656
43	70	17,785	764,755
35	60	14,197	496,895
40	50	10,606	424,240
45	40	7,558	340,110
58	20	3,710	215,180
85 Sloops, bombs, and fireships, one another		2,000	170,000
Cost			3,266,786
Remains for guns			229,214
Total			3500,000

No country on the globe is so happily situated, or internally capable of raising a fleet as America. Tar, timber, iron, and cordage are her natural produce. We need go abroad for nothing. Whereas the Dutch, who make large profits by hiring out their ships of war to the Spaniards and Portuguese, are obliged to import most of their materials they use. We ought to view the building a fleet as an article of commerce, it being the natural manufactory of this country. It is the best money we can lay out. A navy when finished is worth more than it cost. And is that nice point in national policy, in which commerce and protection are united. Let us build; if we want them not, we can sell; and by that means replace our paper currency with ready gold and silver.

In point of manning a fleet, people in general run into great errors; it is not necessary that one fourth part should be sailors. The privateer Terrible, Captain Death, stood the hottest engagement of any ship last war, yet had not twenty sailors on board, though her complement of men was upwards of two hundred. A few able and social sailors will soon instruct a sufficient number of active landsmen in the common work of a ship. Wherefore, we never can be more capable to begin on maritime matters than now, while our timber is standing, our fisheries blocked up, and our sailors and shipwrights out of employ. Men of war of seventy and eighty guns were built forty years ago in New-England, and why not the same now? Ship-building is America's greatest pride, and in which she will in time excel the whole world. The great empires of the east are mostly inland, and consequently excluded from the possibility of rivalling her. Africa is in a state of barbarism; and no power in Europe, hath either such an extent of coast, or such an internal supply of materials. Where nature hath given the one, she has withheld the other; to America only hath she been liberal of both. The vast empire of Russia is almost shut out from the sea: wherefore, her boundless forests, her tar, iron, and cordage are only articles of commerce.

In point of safety, ought we to be without a fleet? We are not the little people now, which we were sixty years ago; at that time we might have trusted our property in the streets, or fields rather; and slept securely without locks or bolts to our doors or windows. The case now is altered, and our methods of defence ought to improve with our increase of property. A common pirate, twelve months ago, might have come up the Delaware, and laid the city of Philadelphia under instant contribution, for what sum he pleased; and the same might have happened to other places. Nay, any daring fellow, in a brig of fourteen or sixteen guns, might have robbed the whole continent, and carried off half a million of money. These are circumstances which demand our attention, and point out the necessity of naval protection.

Some, perhaps, will say, that after we have made it up with Britain, she will protect us. Can we be so unwise as to mean, that she shall keep a navy in our harbours for that purpose? Common sense will tell us, that the power which hath endeavoured to subdue us, is of all others the most improper to defend us. Conquest may be effected under the pretence of friendship; and ourselves after a long and brave resistance, be at last cheated into slavery. And if her ships are not to be admitted into our harbours, I would ask, how is she to protect us? A navy three or four thousand miles off can be of little use, and on sudden emergencies, none at all. Wherefore, if we must hereafter protect ourselves, why not do it for ourselves? Why doit for another?

The English list of ships of war, is long and formidable, but not a tenth part of them are at any one time fit for service, numbers of them not in being; yet their names are pompously continued in the list, if only a plank be left of the ship: and not a fifth part of such as are fit for service, can be spared on any one station at one time. The East and West Indies, Mediterranean, Africa, and other parts over which Britain extends her claim, make large demands upon her navy. From a mixture of prejudice and inattention, we have contracted a false notion respecting the navy of England, and have talked as if we should have the whole of it to encounter at once, and for that reason, supposed that we must have one as large; which not being instantly practicable, have been made use of by a set of disguised tories to discourage our beginning thereon. Nothing can be farther from truth than this; for if America had only a twentieth part of the naval force of Britain, she would be by far an over match for her; because, as we neither have, nor claim any foreign dominion, our whole force would be employed on our own coast, where we should, in the long run, have two to one the advantage of those who had three or four thousand miles to sail over, before they could attack us, and the same distance to return in order to refit and recruit. And although Britain, by her fleet, hath a check over our trade to Europe, we have as large a one over her trade to the West Indies, which, by laying in the neighbourhood of the continent, is entirely at its mercy.

Some method might be fallen on to keep up a naval force in time of peace, if we should not judge it necessary to support a constant navy. If premiums were to be given to merchants, to build and employ in their service, ships mounted with twenty, thirty, forty, or fifty guns, (the premiums to be in proportion to the loss of bulk to the merchants) fifty or sixty of those ships, with a few guard ships on constant duty, would keep up a sufficient navy, and that without burdening ourselves with the evil so loudly complained of in England, of suffering their fleet, in time of peace to lie rotting in the docks. To unite the sinews of commerce and defence is sound policy; for when our strength and our riches, play into each other's hand, we need fear no external enemy.

In almost every article of defence we abound. Hemp flourishes even to rankness, so that we need not want cordage. Our iron is superior to that of other countries. Our small arms equal to any in the world. Cannon we can cast at pleasure. Saltpetre and gunpowder we are every day producing. Our knowledge is hourly improving. Resolution is our inherent character, and courage hath never yet forsaken us. Wherefore, what is it that we want? Why is it that we hesitate? From Britain we can expect nothing but ruin. If she is once admitted to the government of America again, this Continent will not be worth living in. Jealousies will be always arising; insurrections will be constantly happening; and who will go forth to quell them? Who will venture his life to reduce his own countrymen to a foreign obedience? The difference between Pennsylvania and Connecticut, respecting some unlocated lands, shows the insignificance of a British government, and fully proves, that nothing but Continental authority can regulate Continental matters.

Another reason why the present time is preferable to all others, is, that the fewer our numbers are, the more land there is yet unoccupied, which instead of being lavished by the king on his worthless dependants, may be hereafter applied, not only to the discharge of the present debt, but to the constant support of government. No nation under heaven hath such an advantage as this.

The infant state of the Colonies, as it is called, so far from being against, is an argument in favor of independance. We are sufficiently numerous, and were we more so, we might be less united. It is a matter worthy of observation, that the more a country is peopled, the smaller their armies are. In military numbers, the ancients far exceeded the moderns: and the reason is evident. For trade being the consequence of population, men become too much absorbed thereby to attend to anything else. Commerce diminishes the spirit, both of patriotism and military defence. And history sufficiently informs us, that the bravest achievements were always accomplished in the non-age of a nation. With the increase of commerce, England hath lost its spirit. The city of London, notwithstanding its numbers, submits to continued insults with the patience of a coward. The more men have to lose, the less willing are they to venture. The rich are in general slaves to fear, and submit to courtly power with the trembling duplicity of a Spaniel.

Youth is the seed time of good habits, as well in nations as in individuals. It might be difficult, if not impossible, to form the Continent into one government half a century hence. The vast variety of interests, occasioned by an increase of trade and population, would create confusion. Colony would be against colony. Each being able might scorn each other's assistance: and while the proud and foolish gloried in their little distinctions, the wise would lament, that the union had not been formed before. Wherefore, the present time is the true time for establishing it. The intimacy which is contracted in infancy, and the friendship which is formed in misfortune, are, of all others, the most lasting and unalterable. Our present union is marked with both these characters: we are young and we have been distressed; but our concord hath withstood our troubles, and fixes a memorable area for posterity to glory in.

The present time, likewise, is that peculiar time, which never happens to a nation but once, viz. the time of forming itself into a government. Most nations have let slip the opportunity, and by that means have been compelled to receive laws from their conquerors, instead of making laws for themselves. First, they had a king, and then a form of government; whereas, the articles or charter of government, should be formed first, and men delegated to execute them afterward: but from the errors of other nations, let us learn wisdom, and lay hold of the present opportunity—to begin government at the right end.

When William the Conqueror subdued England, he gave them law at the point of the sword; and until we consent that the seat of government in America, be legally and authoritatively occupied, we shall be in danger of having it filled by some fortunate ruffian, who may treat us in the same manner, and then, where will be our freedom? where our property?

As to religion, I hold it to be the indispensable duty of all government, to protect all conscientious professors thereof, and I know of no other business which government hath to do therewith, Let a man throw aside that narrowness of soul, that selfishness of principle, which the niggards of all professions are so unwilling to part with, and he will be at once delivered of his fears on that head. Suspicion is the companion of mean souls, and the bane of all good society. For myself I fully and conscientiously believe, that it is the will of the Almighty, that there should be diversity of religious opinions among us: It affords a larger field for our Christian kindness. Were we all of one way of thinking, our religious dispositions would want matter for probation; and on this liberal principle, I look on the various denominations among us, to be like children of the same family, differing only, in what is called their Christian names.

Earlier in this work, I threw out a few thoughts on the propriety of a Continental Charter, (for I only presume to offer hints, not plans) and in this place, I take the liberty of rementioning the subject, by observing, that a charter is to be understood as a bond of solemn obligation, which the whole enters into, to support the right of every separate part, whether of religion, personal freedom, or property. A firm bargain and a right reckoning make long friends.

In a former page I likewise mentioned the necessity of a large and equal representation; and there is no political matter which more deserves our attention. A small number of electors, or a small number of representatives, are equally dangerous. But if the number of the representatives be not only small, but unequal, the danger is increased. As an instance of this, I mention the following; when the Associators petition was before the House of Assembly of Pennsylvania; twenty-eight members only were present, all the Bucks county members, being eight, voted against it, and had seven of the Chester members done the same, this whole province had been governed by two counties only, and this danger it is always exposed to. The unwarrantable stretch likewise, which that house made in their last sitting, to gain an undue authority over the delegates of that province, ought to warn the people at large, how they trust power out of their own hands. A set of instructions for the Delegates were put together, which in point of sense and business would have dishonoured a schoolboy, and after being approved by a few, a very few without doors, were carried into the House, and there passed in behalf of the whole colony; whereas, did the whole colony know, with what ill-will that House hath entered on some necessary public measures, they would not hesitate a moment to think them unworthy of such a trust.

Immediate necessity makes many things convenient, which if continued would grow into oppressions. Expedience and right are different things. When the calamities of America required a consultation, there was no method so ready, or at that time so proper, as to appoint persons from the several Houses of Assembly for that purpose and the wisdom with which they have proceeded hath preserved this continent from ruin. But as it is more than probable that we shall never be without a congress, every well-wisher to good order, must own, that the mode for choosing members of that body, deserves consideration. And I put it as a question to those, who make a study of mankind, whether representation and election is not too great a power for one and the same body of men to possess? When we are planning for posterity, we ought to remember, that virtue is not hereditary.

It is from our enemies that we often gain excellent maxims, and are frequently surprised into reason by their mistakes, Mr. Cornwall (one of the Lords of the Treasury) treated the petition of the New-York Assembly with contempt, because that House, he said, consisted but of twenty-six members, which trifling number, he argued, could not with decency be put for the whole. We thank him for his involuntary honesty. [1]

To conclude: However strange it may appear to some, or however unwilling they may be to think so, matters not, but many strong and striking reasons may be given, to show, that nothing can settle our affairs so expeditiously as an open and determined declaration for independance. Some of which are:

First. It is the custom of nations, when any two are at war, for some other powers, not engaged in the quarrel, to step in as mediators, and bring about the preliminaries of a peace: but while America calls herself the Subject of Great Britain, no power, however well disposed she may be, can offer her mediation. Wherefore, in our present state we may quarrel on for ever.

Secondly. It is unreasonable to suppose, that France or Spain will give us any kind of assistance, if we mean only to make use of that assistance for the purpose of repairing the breach, and strengthening the connection between Britain and America; because, those powers would be sufferers by the consequences.

Thirdly. While we profess ourselves the subjects of Britain, we must, in the eye of foreign nations, be considered as rebels. The

---

[1]   Those who would fully understand of what great consequence a large and equal representation is to a state, should read Burgh's political disquisitions.

precedent is somewhat dangerous to their peace, for men to be in arms under the name of subjects; we on the spot, can solve the paradox: but to unite resistance and subjection, requires an idea much too refined for common understanding.

Fourthly. Were a manifesto to be published, and despatched to foreign courts, setting forth the miseries we have endured, and the peaceable methods we have ineffectually used for redress; declaring, at the same time, that not being able, any longer, to live happily or safely under the cruel disposition of the British court, we had been driven to the necessity of breaking off all connections with her; at the same time, assuring all such courts of our peaceable disposition towards them, and of our desire of entering into trade with them: Such a memorial would produce more good effects to this Continent, than if a ship were freighted with petitions to Britain.

Under our present denomination of British subjects, we can neither be received nor heard abroad: The custom of all courts is against us, and will be so, until, by an independance, we take rank with other nations.

These proceedings may at first appear strange and difficult; but, like all other steps which we have already passed over, will in a little time become familiar and agreeable; and, until an independance is declared, the Continent will feel itself like a man who continues putting off some unpleasant business from day to day, yet knows it must be done, hates to set about it, wishes it over, and is continually haunted with the thoughts of its necessity.

Appendix

SINCE the publication of the first edition of this pamphlet, or rather, on the same day on which it came out, the King's Speech made its appearance in this city. Had the spirit of prophecy directed the birth of this production, it could not have brought it forth, at a more seasonable juncture, or a more necessary time. The bloody mindedness of the one, show the necessity of pursuing the doctrine of the other. Men read by way of revenge. And the Speech instead of terrifying, prepared a way for the manly principles of independance.

Ceremony, and even, silence, from whatever motive they may arise, have a hurtful tendency, when they give the least degree of countenance to base and wicked performances; wherefore, if this maxim be admitted, it naturally follows, that the King's Speech, as being a piece of finished villainy, deserved, and still deserves, a general execration both by the Congress and the people. Yet, as the domestic tranquillity of a nation, depends greatly on the chastity of what may properly be called national manners, it is often better, to pass some things over in silent disdain, than to make use of such new methods of dislike, as might introduce the least innovation, on that guardian of our peace and safety. And, perhaps, it is chiefly owing to this prudent delicacy, that the King's Speech, hath not before now, suffered a public execution. The Speech if it may be called one, is nothing better than a wilful audacious libel against the truth, the common good, and the existence of mankind; and is a formal and pompous method of offering up human sacrifices to the pride of tyrants. But this general massacre of mankind, is one of the privileges, and the certain consequences of Kings; for as nature knows them not, they know not her, and although they are beings of our own creating, they know not us, and are become the gods of their creators. The Speech hath one good quality, which is, that it is not calculated to deceive, neither can we, even if we would, be deceived by it. Brutality and tyranny appear on the face of it. It leaves us at no loss: And every line convinces, even in the moment of reading, that He, who hunts the woods for prey, the naked and untutored Indian, is less a Savage than the King of Britain.

Sir John Dalrymple, the putative father of a whining jesuitical piece, fallaciously called, "The address of the people of ENGLAND to the inhabitants of America," hath, perhaps from a vain supposition, that the people here were to be frightened at the pomp and description of a king, given, (though very unwisely on his part) the real character of the present one: "But," says this writer, "if you are inclined to pay compliments to an administration, which we do not complain of," (meaning the Marquis of Rockingham's at the repeal of the Stamp Act) "it is very unfair in you to withhold them from that prince, by whose NOD ALONE they were permitted to do anything." This is toryism with a witness! Here is idolatry even without a mask: And he who can calmly hear, and digest such doctrine, hath forfeited his claim to rationality an apostate from the order of manhood; and ought to be considered—as one, who hath, not only given up the proper dignity of a man, but sunk himself beneath the rank of animals, and contemptibly crawl through the world like a worm.

However, it matters very little now, what the king of England either says or does; he hath wickedly broken through every moral and human obligation, trampled nature and conscience beneath his feet; and by a steady and constitutional spirit of insolence and cruelty, procured for himself an universal hatred. It is NOW the interest of America to provide for herself. She hath already a large and young family, whom it is more her duty to take care of, than to be granting away her property, to support a power who is become a reproach to the names of men and christians. Ye, whose office it is to watch over the morals of a nation, of whatsoever sect or denomination ye are of, as well as ye, who are more immediately the guardians of the public liberty, if ye wish to preserve your native country uncontaminated by European corruption, ye must in secret wish a separation. But leaving the moral part to private reflection, I shall chiefly confine my farther remarks to the following heads:

First. That it is the interest of America to be separated from Britain.

Secondly. Which is the easiest and most practicable plan, reconciliation or independance? With some occasional remarks.

In support of the first, I could, if I judged it proper, produce the opinion of some of the ablest and most experienced men on this continent; and whose sentiments, on that head, are not yet publicly known. It is in reality a self-evident position: For no nation in a state of foreign dependance, limited in its commerce, and cramped and fettered in its legislative powers, can ever arrive at any material eminence. America doth not yet know what opulence is; and although the progress which she hath made stands unparalleled in the history of other nations, it is but childhood, compared with what she would be capable of arriving at, had she, as she ought to have, the legislative powers in her own hands. England is, at this time, proudly coveting what would do her no good, were she to accomplish it; and the Continent hesitating on a matter, which will be her final ruin if neglected. It is the commerce and not the conquest of America, by which England is to be benefited, and that would in a great measure continue, were the countries as independant of each other as France and Spain; because in many articles, neither can go to a better market. But it is the independance of this country of Britain or any other which is now the main and only object worthy of contention, and which, like all other truths discovered by necessity, will appear clearer and stronger every day.

First. Because it will come to that one time or other.

Secondly. Because the longer it is delayed the harder it will be to accomplish.

I have frequently amused myself both in public and private companies, with silently remarking the specious errors of those who speak without reflecting. And among the many which I have heard, the following seems the most general, viz. that had this rupture happened forty or fifty years hence, instead of now, the Continent would have been more able to have shaken off the dependance. To which I reply, that our military ability at this time, arises from the experience gained in the last war, and which in forty or fifty years time, would have been totally extinct. The Continent, would not, by that time, have had a General, or even a military officer left; and we, or those who may succeed us, would have been as ignorant of martial matters as the ancient Indians: And this single position, closely attended to, will unanswerably prove, that the present time is preferable to all others: The argument turns thus—at the conclusion of the last war, we had experience, but wanted numbers; and forty or fifty years hence, we should have numbers, without experience; wherefore, the proper point of time, must be some particular point between the two extremes, in which a sufficiency of the former remains, and a proper increase of the latter is obtained: And that point of time is the present time.

The reader will pardon this digression, as it does not properly come under the head I first set out with, and to which I again return by the following position, viz.:

Should affairs be patched up with Britain, and she to remain the governing and sovereign power of America, (which as matters are now circumstanced, is giving up the point entirely) we shall deprive ourselves of the very means of sinking the debt we have or may contract. The value of the back lands which some of the provinces are clandestinely deprived of, by the unjust extension of the limits of Canada, valued only at five pounds sterling per hundred acres, amount to upwards of twenty-five millions, Pennsylvania currency; and the quit-rents at one penny sterling per acre, to two millions yearly.

It is by the sale of those lands that the debt may be sunk, without burden to any, and the quit-rent reserved thereon, will always lessen, and in time, will wholly support the yearly expense of government. It matters not how long the debt is in paying, so that the lands when sold be applied to the discharge of it, and for the execution of which, the Congress for the time being, will be the continental trustees.

I proceed now to the second head, viz. Which is the earliest and most practicable plan, reconciliation or independance? With some occasional remarks.

He who takes nature for his guide is not easily beaten out of his argument, and on that ground, I answer generally—That INDEPENDANCE being a SINGLE SIMPLE LINE, contained within ourselves; and reconciliation, a matter exceedingly perplexed and complicated, and in which, a treacherous capricious court is to interfere, gives the answer without a doubt.

The present state of America is truly alarming to every man who is capable of reflexion. Without law, without government, without any other mode of power than what is founded on, and granted by courtesy. Held together by an unexampled concurrence of sentiment, which is nevertheless subject to change, and which every secret enemy is endeavoring to dissolve. Our present condition, is, legislation without law; wisdom without a plan; a constitution without a name; and, what is strangely astonishing, perfect independance contending for dependance. The instance is without a precedent; the case never existed before; and who can tell what may be the event? The property of no man is secure in the present unbraced system of things. The mind of the multitude is left at random, and feeling no fixed object before them, they pursue such as fancy or opinion starts.

Nothing is criminal; there is no such thing as treason; wherefore, every one thinks himself at liberty to act as he pleases. The tories dared not to have assembled offensively, had they known that their lives, by that act were forfeited to the laws of the state. A line of distinction should be drawn, between English soldiers taken in battle, and inhabitants of America taken in arms. The first are prisoners, but the latter traitors. The one forfeits his liberty the other his head.

Notwithstanding our wisdom, there is a visible feebleness in some of our proceedings which gives encouragement to dissensions. The Continental Belt is too loosely buckled. And if something is not done in time, it will be too late to do any thing, and we shall fall into a state, in which, neither reconciliation nor independance will be practicable. The king and his worthless adherents are got at their old game of dividing the continent, and there are not wanting among us Printers, who will be busy spreading specious falsehoods. The artful and hypocritical letter which appeared a few months ago in two of the New York papers, and likewise in two others, is an evidence that there are men who want either judgment or honesty.

It is easy getting into holes and corners and talking of reconciliation: But do such men seriously consider, how difficult the task is, and how dangerous it may prove, should the Continent divide thereon. Do they take within their view, all the various orders of men whose situation and circumstances, as well as their own, are to be considered therein. Do they put themselves in the place of the sufferer whose all is already gone, and of the soldier, who hath quitted all for the defence of his country. If their ill judged moderation be suited to their own private situations only, regardless of others, the event will convince them, that "they are reckoning without their Host."

Put us, says some, on the footing we were in the year 1763: To which I answer, the request is not now in the power of Britain to comply with, neither will she propose it; but if it were, and even should be granted, I ask, as a reasonable question, By what means is such a corrupt and faithless court to be kept to its engagements?

Another parliament, nay, even the present, may hereafter repeal the obligation, on the pretence of its being violently obtained, or unwisely granted; and in that case, Where is our redress? No going to law with nations; cannon are the barristers of Crowns; and the sword, not of justice, but of war, decides the suit.

To be on the footing of 1763, it is not sufficient, that the laws only be put on the same state, but, that our circumstances, likewise, be put on the same state; our burnt and destroyed towns repaired or built up, our private losses made good, our public debts (contracted for defence) discharged; otherwise, we shall be millions worse than we were at that enviable period. Such a request had it been complied with a year ago, would have won the heart and soul of the Continent—but now it is too late, "the Rubicon is passed."

Besides the taking up arms, merely to enforce the repeal of a pecuniary law, seems as unwarrantable by the divine law, and as repugnant to human feelings, as the taking up arms to enforce obedience thereto. The object, on either side, doth not justify the ways and means; for the lives of men are too valuable to be cast away on such trifles. It is the violence which is done and threatened to our persons; the destruction of our property by an armed force; the invasion of our country by fire and sword, which conscientiously qualifies the use of arms: And the instant, in which such a mode of defence became necessary, all subjection to Britain ought to have ceased; and the independancy of America should have been considered, as dating its aera from, and published by, the first musket that was fired against her. This line is a line of consistency; neither drawn by caprice, nor extended by ambition; but produced by a chain of events, of which the colonies were not the authors.

I shall conclude these remarks, with the following timely and well intended hints. We ought to reflect, that there are three different ways by which an independancy may hereafter be effected; and that one of those three, will one day or other, be the fate of America, viz. By the legal voice of the people in Congress; by a military power; or by a mob: It may not always happen that our soldiers are citizens, and the multitude a body of reasonable men; virtue, as I have already remarked, is not hereditary, neither is it perpetual. Should an independancy be brought about by the first of those means, we have every opportunity and every encouragement before us, to form the noblest, purest constitution on the face of the earth. We have it in our power to begin the world over again. A situation, similar to the present, hath not happened since the days of Noah until now. The birthday of a new world is at hand, and a race of men perhaps as numerous as all

Europe contains, are to receive their portion of freedom from the event of a few months. The reflection is awful—and in this point of view, how trifling, how ridiculous, do the little, paltry cavillings, of a few weak or interested men appear, when weighed against the business of a world.

Should we neglect the present favourable and inviting period, and an independance be hereafter effected by any other means, we must charge the consequence to ourselves, or to those rather, whose narrow and prejudiced souls, are habitually opposing the measure, without either inquiring or reflecting. There are reasons to be given in support of independance, which men should rather privately think of, than be publicly told of. We ought not now to be debating whether we shall be independant or not, but, anxious to accomplish it on a firm, secure, and honorable basis, and uneasy rather that it is not yet began upon. Every day convinces us of its necessity. Even the tories (if such beings yet remain among us) should, of all men, be the most solicitous to promote it; for, as the appointment of committees at first, protected them from popular rage, so, a wise and well established form of government, will be the only certain means of continuing it securely to them. Wherefore, if they have not virtue enough to be Whigs, they ought to have prudence enough to wish for independance.

In short, independance is the only bond that can tie and keep us together. We shall then see our object, and our ears will be legally shut against the schemes of an intriguing, as well as a cruel enemy. We shall then too, be on a proper footing, to treat with Britain; for there is reason to conclude, that the pride of that court, will be less hurt by treating with the American states for terms of peace, than with those, whom she denominates, "rebellious subjects," for terms of accommodation. It is our delaying it that encourages her to hope for conquest, and our backwardness tends only to prolong the war. As we have, without any good effect therefrom, withheld our trade to obtain a redress of our grievances, let us now try the alternative, by independantly redressing them ourselves, and then offering to open the trade. The mercantile and reasonable part of England will be still with us; because, peace with trade, is preferable to war without it. And if this offer be not accepted, other courts may be applied to.

On these grounds I rest the matter. And as no offer hath yet been made to refute the doctrine contained in the former editions of this pamphlet, it is a negative proof, that either the doctrine cannot be refuted, or, that the party in favour of it are too numerous to be opposed. Wherefore, instead of gazing at each other with suspicious or doubtful curiosity; let each of us, hold out to his neighbour the hearty hand of friendship, and unite in drawing a line, which, like an act of oblivion, shall bury in forgetfulness every former dissension. Let the names of Whig and Tory be extinct; and let none other be heard among us, than those of a good citizen, an open and resolute friend,and a virtuous supporter of the RIGHTS of MANKIND and of the FREE AND INDEPENDANT STATES OF AMERICA.

Epistle to Quakers

To the Representatives of the Religious Society of the People called Quakers, or to so many of them as were concerned in publishing the late piece, entitled "THE ANCIENT TESTIMONY and PRINCIPLES of the People called QUAKERS renewed, with Respect to the KING and GOVERNMENT, and touching the COMMOTIONS now prevailing in these and other parts of AMERICA addressed to the PEOPLE IN GENERAL."

The Writer of this, is one of those few, who never dishonours religion either by ridiculing, or cavilling at any denomination whatsoever. To God, and not to man, are all men accountable on the score of religion. Wherefore, this epistle is not so properly addressed to you as a religious, but as a political body, dabbling in matters, which the professed Quietude of your Principles instruct you not to meddle with.

As you have, without a proper authority for so doing, put yourselves in the place of the whole body of the Quakers, so, the writer of this, in order to be on an equal rank with yourselves, is under the necessity, of putting himself in the place of all those who approve the very writings and principles, against which your testimony is directed: And he hath chosen this singular situation, in order that you might discover in him, that presumption of character which you cannot see in yourselves. For neither he nor you can have any claim or title to political representation.

When men have departed from the right way, it is no wonder that they stumble and fall. And it is evident from the manner in which ye have managed your testimony, that politics, (as a religious body of men) is not your proper walk; for however well adapted it might appear to you, it is, nevertheless, a jumble of good and bad put unwisely together, and the conclusion drawn therefrom, both unnatural and unjust.

The two first pages, (and the whole doth not make four) we give you credit for, and expect the same civility from you, because the love and desire of peace is not confined to Quakerism, it is the natural, as well the religious wish of all denominations of men. And on this ground, as men labouring to establish an Independant Constitution of our own, do we exceed all others in our hope, end, and aim. Our plan is peace for ever. We are tired of contention with Britain, and can see no real end to it but in a final separation. We act consistently, because for the sake of introducing an endless and uninterrupted peace, do we bear the evils and burdens of the present day. We are endeavoring, and will steadily continue to endeavour, to separate and dissolve a connection which hath already filled our land with blood; and which, while the name of it remains, will be the fatal cause of future mischiefs to both countries.

We fight neither for revenge nor conquest; neither from pride nor passion; we are not insulting the world with our fleets and armies, nor ravaging the globe for plunder. Beneath the shade of our own vines are we attacked; in our own houses, and on our own lands, is the violence committed against us. We view our enemies in the character of highwaymen and housebreakers, and having no defence for ourselves in the civil law, are obliged to punish them by the military one, and apply the sword, in the very case, where you have before now, applied the halter.

Perhaps we feel for the ruined and insulted sufferers in all and every part of the continent, with a degree of tenderness which hath not yet made its way into some of your bosoms. But be ye sure that ye mistake not the cause and ground of your Testimony. Call not coldness of soul, religion; nor put the bigot in the place of the Christian.

O ye partial ministers of your own acknowledged principles. If the bearing arms be sinful, the first going to war must be more so, by all the difference between wilful attack, and unavoidable defence.

Wherefore, if ye really preach from conscience, and mean not to make a political hobby-horse of your religion convince the world thereof, by proclaiming your doctrine to our enemies, for they likewise bear ARMS. Give us proof of your sincerity by publishing it at St. James's, to the commanders in chief at Boston, to the Admirals and Captains who are piratically ravaging our coasts, and to all the murdering miscreants who are acting in authority under him whom ye profess to serve. Had ye the honest soul of barclay ye would preach repentance to your king; Ye would tell the royal tyrant his sins, and warn him of eternal ruin.[1] Ye would not spend your partial invectives

---

[1] "Thou hast tasted of prosperity and adversity; thou knowest what it is to be banished thy native country, to be over-ruled as well as to rule, and set upon the throne; and being oppressed thou hast reason to know how hateful the oppressor is both to God and man: If after all these warnings and advertisements, thou dost not turn unto the Lord with all thy heart, but forget him who remembered thee in thy distress, and give up

against the injured and the insulted only, but like faithful ministers, would cry aloud and spare none. Say not that ye are persecuted, neither endeavour to make us the authors of that reproach, which, ye are bringing upon yourselves; for we testify unto all men, that we do not complain against you because ye are Quakers, but because ye pretend to be and are NOT Quakers.

Alas! It seems by the particular tendency of some part of your testimony, and other parts of your conduct, as if all sin was reduced to, and comprehended in the act of bearing arms, and that by the people only. Ye appear to us, to have mistaken party for conscience; because the general tenor of your actions wants uniformity. And it is exceedingly difficult to us to give credit to many of your pretended scruples; because we see them made by the same men, who, in the very instant that they are exclaiming against the mammon of this world, are nevertheless, hunting after it with a step as steady as Time, and an appetite as keen as Death.

The quotation which ye have made from Proverbs, in the third

（续）_____

thyself to follow lust and vanity, surely great will be thy condemnation. Against which snare, as well as the temptation of those who may or do feed thee, and prompt thee to evil, the most excellent and prevalent remedy will be, to apply thyself to that light of Christ which shineth in thy conscience, and which neither can, nor will flatter thee, nor suffer thee to be at ease in thy sins." —Barclay's Address to Charles II.

page of your testimony, that, "when a man's ways please the Lord, he maketh even his enemies to be at peace with him"; is very unwisely chosen on your part; because, it amounts to a proof, that the king's ways (whom ye are desirous of supporting) do not please the Lord, otherwise, his reign would be in peace.

I now proceed to the latter part of your testimony, and that, for which all the foregoing seems only an introduction, viz:

"It hath ever been our judgment and principle, since we were called to profess the light of Christ Jesus, manifested in our consciences unto this day, that the setting up and putting down kings and governments, is God's peculiar prerogative; for causes best known to himself: And that it is not our business to have any hand or contrivance therein; nor to be busy-bodies above our station, much less to plot and contrive the ruin, or overturn of any of them, but to pray for the king, and safety of our nation, and good of all men: That we may live a peaceable and quiet life, in all godliness and honesty; under the government which god is pleased to set over us." If these are really your principles why do ye not abide by them? Why do ye not leave that, which ye call God's Work, to be managed by himself? These very principles instruct you to wait with patience and humility, for the event of all public measures, and to receive that event as the divine will towards you.

Wherefore, what occasion is there for your political testimony if you fully believe what it contains? And the very publishing it proves, that either, ye do not believe what ye profess, or have not virtue enough to practise what ye believe.

The principles of Quakerism have a direct tendency to make a man the quiet and inoffensive subject of any, and every government which is set over him. And if the setting up and putting down of kings and governments is God's peculiar prerogative, he most certainly will not be robbed thereof by us: wherefore, the principle itself leads you to approve of every thing, which ever happened, or may happen to kings as being his work. Oliver cromwell thanks you. Charles, then, died not by the hands of man; and should the present proud imitator of him, come to the same untimely end, the writers and publishers of the Testimony, are bound by the doctrine it contains, to applaud the fact. Kings are not taken away by miracles, neither are changes in governments brought about by any other means than such as are common and human; and such as we are now using. Even the dispersion of the Jews, though foretold by our Saviour, was effected by arms. Wherefore, as ye refuse to be the means on one side, ye ought not to be meddlers on the other; but to wait the issue in silence; and unless ye can produce divine authority, to prove, that the Almighty who hath created and placed this new world, at the greatest distance it could possibly stand, east and west, from every part of the old, doth, nevertheless, disapprove of its being independant of the corrupt and abandoned court of Britain, unless I say, ye can show this, how can ye on the ground of your principles, justify the exciting and stirring up the people "firmly to unite in the abhorrence of all such writings, and measures, as evidence a desire and design to break off the happy connection we have hitherto enjoyed, with the kingdom of Great-Britain, and our just and necessary subordination to the king, and those who are lawfully placed in authority under him." What a slap in the face is here! The men, who in the very paragraph before, have quietly and passively resigned up the ordering, altering, and disposal of kings and governments, into the hands of God, are now recalling their principles, and putting in for a share of the business. Is it possible, that the conclusion, which is here justly quoted, can any ways follow from the doctrine laid down? The inconsistency is too glaring not to be seen; the absurdity too great not to be laughed at; and such as could only have been made by those, whose understandings were darkened by the narrow and crabby spirit of a despairing political party; for ye are not to be considered as the whole body of the Quakers but only as a factional and fractional part thereof.

Here ends the examination of your testimony; (which I call upon no man to abhor, as ye have done, but only to read and judge of fairly;) to which I subjoin the following remark; "That the setting up and putting down of kings," most certainly mean, the making him a king, who is yet not so, and the making him no king who is already one. And pray what hath this to do in the present case? We neither mean to set up nor to pull down, neither to make nor to unmake, but to have nothing to do with them. Wherefore, your testimony in whatever light it is viewed serves only to dishonor your judgement, and for many other reasons had better have been let alone than published.

First, Because it tends to the decrease and reproach of all religion whatever, and is of the utmost danger to society, to make it a party in political disputes.

Secondly, Because it exhibits a body of men, numbers of whom disavow the publishing political testimonies, as being concerned therein and approvers thereof.

Thirdly, because it hath a tendency to undo that continental harmony and friendship which yourselves by your late liberal and charitable donations hath lent a hand to establish; and the preservation of which, is of the utmost consequence to us all.

And here, without anger or resentment I bid you farewell.

Sincerely wishing, that as men and Christians, ye may always fully and uninterruptedly enjoy every civil and religious right; and be, in your turn, the means of securing it to others; but that the example which ye have unwisely set, of mingling religion with politics, may be disavowed and reprobated by every inhabitant of America.

《国民阅读经典》已出书目

龚艳译　定价：32 元

国富论　[英国]亚当·斯密著　谢祖钧译　定价：58 元

朝花夕拾（典藏对照本）鲁迅原著　周作人解说　止庵编订
　定价：16 元

金刚经·心经释义　王孺童译注　定价：38 元

中国哲学史大纲　胡适著　定价：34 元

圣经的故事　[美]房龙著　张稷译　定价：35 元

大学中庸译注　王文锦译注　定价：24 元

梦的解析　[奥]弗洛伊德著　高申春译　车文博审订
　定价：36.00 元

乡土中国[插图本]　费孝通著　定价：19.00 元

道德经讲义　王孺童讲解　定价：20.00 元

歌德谈话录　[德]爱克曼辑录　朱光潜译　定价：26.00 元

毛泽东诗词欣赏[插图典藏本]　周振甫著　定价：26.00 元